Dismissal Doesn't Have to Be Difficult

What Every Administrator and Supervisor Should Know

Chet H. Elder

ScarecrowEducation
Lanham, Maryland • Toronto • Oxford
2004

Published in the United States of America
by ScarecrowEducation
An imprint of The Rowman & Littlefield Publishing Group, Inc.
4501 Forbes Boulevard, Suite 200, Lanham, Maryland 20706
www.scaroweducation.com

PO Box 317
Oxford
OX2 9RU, UK

British Library Cataloguing in Publication Information Available

Library of Congress Cataloging-in-Publication Data

Elder, Chet H. (Chet Harry), 1942–
  Dismissal doesn't have to be difficult : what every administrator and
supervisor should know / Chet H. Elder.
    p. cm.
  Includes bibliographical references (p.   ) and index.
  ISBN 1-57886-099-7 (pbk. : alk. paper)
  1. Teachers—Dismissal of—United States. 2. Teachers—Rating of—
United States. I. Title.
LB2836 .E53 2004
371.14'4—dc22
                                                    2003023555

∞™ The paper used in this publication meets the minimum requirements of
American National Standard for Information Sciences—Permanence of
Paper for Printed Library Materials, ANSI/NISO Z39.48-1992.
Manufactured in the United States of America.

Contents

Foreword

"You can observe a lot by watching." Yogi Berra was right, and for thirty-two years, Chet H. Elder watched and learned all about the people problems involved in the discipline and discharge of teachers. His observations and experiences recorded in this valuable book are the culmination of those years as a spirited and sophisticated teacher advocate.

Now officially "retired," today Elder represents the management side of the education equation. He shares with you the techniques, tips, and even traps he learned and used effectively over the years as UniServ director for the Maryland State Teacher's Association (MSTA) and as assistant executive director of the Delaware State Education Association (DSEA). In those jobs he interacted with hundreds of teachers and administrators in nearly every school district in the two states, learning both sides' vulnerable spots. Now, boards of education, superintendents, and administrators are consulting with him to share his knowledge.

Elder earned his bachelor's and master's degrees in education, and he is fully certificated as a principal and supervisor in both Maryland and Delaware. His aggressive representation of teachers in more than thirty different school districts provides unique credentials to give professional advice to school management in the field of teacher evaluation, discipline, and dismissal. From long hours and days at the collective bargaining table to handling controversial teacher grievances to appearances in local courts, state courts, and federal courts, and before school boards, state boards, arbitrators, and legislatures in two states, his experience was matched by his success. He has been recognized by his peers and his opponents (including me) as one of the best UniServ directors in the state and the nation.

Chet Elder thus captures a unique perspective on the pattern of administrator and union behavior and the myriad of errors and omissions on both sides of the disputes. Ironically, he says the final results are almost always predictable. They are born out of a lack of knowledge, training, and proper action.

From Chet's standpoint as a sincere believer in the cause of public education, this conclusion was and still is cause for alarm. His workshops and this book should change all of that. Learning the tactics of this professional who spent a career working to overturn teacher evaluation and discipline decisions as an employer is the way to make future judgments stick.

To sum up, this dynamic book provides you with the confidence to carry out one of the most important functions of management's job: evaluation of teachers. As Chet says, "You will be able to dismiss and never miss a wink of sleep at night." I know, because as the legal representative of many boards of education and county superintendents, it was my dubious honor on many occasions to bargain, process grievances, and litigate against him and his teachers organizations. He gave me "nightmares" on more than one occasion.

A. Samuel Cook
Labor and employee relations counsel to public and private sector management (former chairman of the Labor and Employment Law Department of the Venable, Baetjerd & Howard law firm based in Baltimore and Washington, D.C.)

CHAPTER 1

Dismissal Doesn't Have to Be Difficult

Making Dismissals Simple, Professional, and Positive

Ladies and gentlemen, start your engines. You are about to experience a paradigm shift at speeds greater than the race cars at the Indianapolis 500. The pages you are about to read will change your belief system forever. You will learn that getting rid of incompetent teachers isn't such a vexing problem after all. Everything you've been taught about teacher tenure will be turned upside down. By the time you reach the last page of this book, you will be awakened to a new reality. You will be enlightened by the truth, and you will never look back to the days of gloom and doom when you believed you were stuck with a poor teacher forever.

This book takes the exact opposite position of most previously published works on this hot topic. Time and again you have read published articles—indeed, even books—telling you that it is virtually impossible to dismiss a tenured teacher, especially for ineffective teaching. You have been indoctrinated to believe that it takes an inordinate amount of time and a mountain of evidence to sustain such an action. But this author will bring you a new realization that *dismissal doesn't have to be difficult!* As Gandhi put it, "Just because you're the lone voice in the wilderness, it doesn't mean you are wrong."

I won't bore you with fancy educational jargon and buzz words. Truth be told, I never really understood much of it anyway. I am simply going to share with you what I know, not what I think. These pages are backed up by thirty-two years of hard experience in the trenches of school labor relations, not from behind some desk in a swank office filled with oak furniture and self-congratulatory plaques on the wall. So sit back now. Fasten your seat belt. You're about to blast off into a whole new educational lifestyle. You might say we're going to make sure that "no administrator is left behind."

Dismissing a teacher does not have to be a gut-wrenching experience. The entire thrust of this project is to make the process as stress-free as possible. This is serious business, to be sure. We aren't suggesting that it be taken lightly. On the other hand we believe the dismissal process should follow the KISS theory: keep it simple, stupid! Finding its roots in Occam's Razor back in the 1300s, the KISS theory has been around for a long time. It is the perfect antidote to the dreaded dismissal depression that all principals and supervisors suffer. No need for Prozac.

This book is based on a dual-track theory combining KISS with the reality that dismissing mediocre or incompetent employees is often the best thing that ever happened to them. They actually leave with a feeling of relief. In fact, you help them depart with a good-bye kiss—in a professional sense, of course. Research done on employees who had been terminated proves this to be the case. Generally, they end up with better-paying jobs, more satisfying careers, and a new sense of enthusiasm and contentment. In short, they are happy again.

You see, most teachers who are doing an unsatisfactory job know it, and they are perfectly miserable in their current position. Now, don't expect them to come running up to you and admit it, but deep down inside they know. And when the ax falls, they breathe a big sigh of relief. The irony is that most administrators don't know the research or don't believe it, and they dread the very thought of that horrible monster: dismissal.

A CASE IN POINT

Let's take a look at Pete. He came to school every day at seven to finish preparing for the day's lessons. He stayed until six every night to wrap things up. He never turned in a report late, and his lesson plans were textbook-perfect. He was always the first to help out with those extra duties. Walk by his classroom, and you could hear a pin drop. Start a new reading program, and he would support it enthusiastically. Most would say he was the most dedicated member of our staff. But he couldn't control his temper. Every year the kids would get to him, he would grab someone, and I would be defending Pete before the board. After about ten years of this pattern, he went too far and the principal bit the bullet. It was obvious that we couldn't win this time. Pete decided to hang it up. We met at the board office, and he turned in his letter of resignation and retreated to a conference room. He looked at me, took a very deep breath, smiled, shook my hand, and said, "I feel like a ton of bricks has been lifted off of my chest. I feel great for the first time in ten years." You could see the stress literally drain from his body. He was relieved and he was happy. It was like he had just been released from prison. In fact, he had.

KEEP IT SIMPLE, STUPID

There's nothing new here. Throughout the pages of this handbook you will find the very essence of the KISS theory: keep it simple, stupid. The more you stick to the point, the more clearly your message is received. The more direct you are in your verbal and written communications, the more you increase your success rate in either solving the problem or making it clear that the consequences will be dismissal. Not surprisingly, the teacher will feel better about the whole process if it is kept simple and direct.

It is surprising, however, to note that this is the number one misconception of virtually every school administrator in America. Everyone thinks that it is so complicated, that it is so difficult, and that you have to be a legal eagle to fire a tenured teacher even if he or she smokes grass in the boiler room. Not so. Think simple. Think KISS and voilà— he or she is gone!

Time and again we witness a convoluted pattern of avoidance behavior, both written and verbal, on the part of the administrator. It almost seems as if the boss is afraid to hurt the teacher's feelings. This approach not only is unfair to the teacher but gives fertile ground for an appeal. Although motivated by a feeling of kindness, it comes across as uncertainty and incompetence.

I recall one elementary school principal who personified this concept. His PTA members requested that teachers display students' work on their bulletin boards, especially on meeting days. He thought this was a great idea, so he brought it up at the next faculty meeting, after which he sent out a memo requesting that all teachers comply. Soon the classrooms were overflowing with examples of the students' finest work. The parents were pleased.

Unfortunately, according to one of the parents, one teacher didn't display a single page of her kid's work, and following the next PTA meeting, the phones began to ring off the hook. To his dismay he found that one of his tenured teachers disagreed with the plan. He urged her to reconsider, but she was adamant in her opposition. The principal politely prodded the teacher by invoking the need to placate the parents and urged her to reconsider. He left the room feeling pretty confident that she would be a team player.

He soon learned that his optimism was merely wishful thinking. The teacher still didn't display her students' work, and the parents were furious. Now the heat was shifted to the principal. These folks wanted action. So, down the hall he marched with the determination of Caesar. "I want to see those bulletin boards filled with your students' work by the end of the day on Friday," he demanded, albeit in a less than ferocious tone. Friday came, and the cupboard was bare. She hadn't put up one single sheet of paper.

Now here's where the story takes an unbelievable twist. Realizing that another PTA meeting was coming up the next week, this mighty leader decided to take the bull by the horns. He would see to it that his policy was implemented. He reviewed his options. They included a letter of reprimand or even some form of discipline, such as suspension. But, by the same token, he was concerned about causing too much controversy with one of his senior teachers, and he wanted to avoid any disruption of staff morale. So, guess what action he took? Believe it or not, over the weekend, he went into the classroom and put up samples of the kids' work on the bulletin boards himself.

KATHY, KATHY, KATHY

Kathy is a good example. She was a twenty-five-year veteran teacher who was being involuntarily transferred and was later fired. Would you believe it—there was not one single unsatisfactory evaluation or obser-vation in her personnel file. Not one. Yet virtually every administrator who ever evaluated her testified that she was incompetent. Even more incredible was the fact that four years after, she won the involuntary transfer appeal because there was no documentation; there was still not one unsatisfactory write-up in her file.

Guess what? She had been observed and evaluated by four different administrators during this four-year period, and they all testified that she was unsatisfactory. Yet, they all practiced the convoluted approach and gave the union a windfall for its very public hearing. Had they practiced the KISS theory, there wouldn't even have been an appeal.

Sadly, Kathy believed for twenty-five years that she was a good teacher. In all of her career, no administrator ever looked her in the eyes and told her the truth. A simple unsatisfactory rating would have saved thousands of dollars in legal fees and millions of points in negative public relations for the school system. More important, it would have protected hundreds of kids from the damage done by an incompetent teacher.

But that was yesterday. Now you have *Dismissal Doesn't Have to Be Difficult*. Just keep it simple, stupid, and everybody comes out smiling!

SAY WHAT YOU MEAN. MEAN WHAT YOU SAY. BUT DON'T SAY IT MEAN

Any competent administrator can dismiss an incompetent teacher any-time. A dismissal proceeding is not warfare. It is a normal process in the course of doing business. It should be done in a way that honors the teacher as a human being. He or she failed to measure up to your ex-pectations for the kids. He or she didn't commit a crime. Therefore, as Woodrow Wilson said, you should "supply light and not heat."

Easier said than done, you say. Not really. There is no need to be nasty or confrontational. In fact, this is the time to put your best foot forward with compassion. Practicing straightforward honesty presented in a pleasant atmosphere will help the KISS theory prevail.

Naturally, the teacher will be tense and defensive. Negativity on your part will only throw gasoline on those flames. It is possible to be nice when delivering bad news. In fact, it is mandatory—the sign of a top-flight administrator. Keep in mind that you're taking this action to improve the quality of education for the kids. We are in the people business. We should set the standard.

Now if all of this sounds a bit too "warm and fuzzy" for you, let me put it in perspective from the union's standpoint. Frequently I would use the attitude of the administrator as my only lever in defending the teacher.

Remember Mark Fuhrman, the detective who became the focus of the O. J. Simpson trial instead of O. J. Simpson? Just switch the issue away from the teacher's inadequacy to the negative attitude and unprofessional treatment by the administration, and guess what—the union wins.

There is a lot more to fair dismissal than simply tacking a pink slip on the classroom door on the Friday before spring break. Dialogue presupposes communication. Communication requires understanding. In short, both parties have to know what's up. Human nature is pretty amazing if you think about it. Most of us know when we're not measuring up. So by a simple process of open and honest dialogue, we begin to knock down the barriers. Straightforward observation and evaluation reporting will guarantee that no teacher is ever shocked and surprised when he or she receives the final word.

Every evaluation is either satisfactory or unsatisfactory, and that message must be crystal clear on every single written evaluation report. Ambiguity can be the union's best friend.

Later in this book, we will discuss in detail the pitfalls of writing too much. For now, however, a word of caution is in order. By focusing on the message you want to convey, you can keep your written verbiage to a minimum while still couching your words in diplomatic terms. In reading hundreds of letters of this nature, it appeared that administrators would write and write and beat around the bush in an effort to assuage the teachers' feelings. In so doing they clouded the issue, filled the pages with ambiguity, and played right into the hands of the union. In reality, these epistles cause confusion in the minds of the teachers. Far too frequently the administrator apparently felt compelled to praise the teacher for his or her positive contributions even though the purpose of the letter was to convey a disciplinary decision.

Perhaps this approach makes the writer feel better about having to deliver the bad news and that somehow these words of praise will soften the blow. Quite honestly, the exact opposite is true. The teacher will resent the inherent conflict in this mixed message.

"If I am deserving of such praise, why are you dismissing me?" will be a typical refrain. Obviously, the union will exploit these inconsistencies and will use the principal's well-intended words to make him or her look indecisive.

A successful dismissal action by an administrator is just like a successful lesson taught by a teacher. It requires preparation and a written lesson plan, complete with written objectives stated in behavioral terms. If you don't have a written plan, you don't have a plan. Based on my observations, administrators frequently entered these situations without much advance thought, let alone detailed written plans. And this was always a formula for disaster.

In my union training sessions, I advised negotiators to spend two to three hours of preparation for each hour at the table. The same is true for administrators preparing for a dismissal action. By using a written plan, you will force yourself to stay on message. What we all learned as student teachers will still serve as a valuable tool in our current professional role: By carefully planning your strategy and then simply following your lesson plan, you will find it much easier to stay focused and to make it through the dismissal process without suffering a panic attack or developing an ulcer.

I observed an interesting phenomenon over the years in dealing with building-level administrators and central office staff. Building-level administrators were much more prone to confrontation than were those at the central office. Principals seemed to feel threatened by a challenge to their authority by the teacher or the union. It became an invasion of their turf, their space, their base of power. As a result, they were more apt to blow their cool. Reacting defensively causes the adrenaline to flow, the blood pressure to rise, and before long your conference has disintegrated into armed combat. You've taken the union bait, lost the high ground, and set yourself up as the target of the union campaign.

Self-control is one of the essential traits of effective leaders according to virtually every prevailing leadership theory. Leaders must realize that their emotions have a strong effect on their employees. Daniel P.

Goleman, in his best-seller *Emotional Intelligence*, notes that top companies choose the person with the greatest self-control. "If you are going to entrust a division to someone, you don't want that someone losing it under stress," Goleman writes. Quite obviously, the same point applies to a school administrator. Having a good written plan of action, and following it, will guarantee that you will avoid this trap. It will put you in control of the agenda. Someone (I think it was I) once said, "He who controls the agenda, controls the outcome." Just remember, your agenda includes coming across as a professional who handles the difficult situations with dignity and respect. Believe me—it will be noticed.

I recall one principal who was faced with a particularly ticklish situation at graduation time when a senior got caught drinking beer. The school policy, of course, prohibited such activity, and the penalty was forfeiture of the graduation ceremonies. What seemed like a simple matter was complicated by the fact that the student's parents were teachers in the same school. The kid was a super student, a good athlete, and never in any trouble before. It was just a graduation party, a one-time slip of good common sense, and he got caught. Mom and Dad and a few other friends on the staff pleaded for special consideration. This principal had a good working relationship with his faculty and was a personal friend of the family. The heat was on.

After wrestling with his conscience, the principal made his decision. The policy would stand. No exceptions would be made. Hard feelings aside, he felt he made the right call. A day or two after graduation another member of the staff stopped by his office to discuss the incident. "Congratulations on having the guts to stand firm on our school policy," she said. "The teachers support you on this. We were all watching to see how you would handle this sticky wicket. We now know we have a principal who will stand behind us and the school rules," she concluded.

Another classic case comes to mind with regard to having a good lesson plan when you're dealing with a grievance or a dismissal conference.

WALLY

Wally was the principal of a large high school in the roughest part of town. He ruled with an iron fist, both the kids and the teachers. Even our union rep was a tad bit frightened of him, and he cautioned that

Wally would be mad as a bear when I got into his office. I had no reason to doubt this assessment.

A naive young female teacher had filed a grievance over an evaluation. It was her first. She was a nervous wreck.

This principal was recognized as the most powerful administrator in the district. Some even said he had more sway than the superintendent, although I know for a fact that the superintendent didn't agree with that assessment. Wally hated being challenged. He seldom was.

All set for the showdown, we walked into his office and there he was, perched behind his throne, uh, I mean desk. Expecting his bombast, I initiated the discussion with small talk. I complimented him on the great football team his school had. Knowing he was a sports enthusiast, I figured that would play to his ego.

To my pleasant surprise, Wally was unprepared. He had no files on his desk, no paperwork, and a contract that looked brand new (a sure clue he hadn't been reading it much). Lo and behold this was his first grievance, and he didn't have a clue. In fact, he wasn't even sure what section of the contract we were citing. His bombast soon turned to sheer frustration, and he blurted out, "Look, I've never had a grievance filed against me before. I don't know what I'm supposed to do!" He went further, "You're the big expert here, and I'm here to learn." Advantage union!

Not one to shy away from a home field advantage, I quickly took control of the agenda, *my* agenda, and thus the outcome of the meeting. Wally took notes like a first-year grad student, and the naive young teacher just filed her nails. Of course, we won the grievance.

But now let me tell you "the rest of the story." Wally had a clear-cut winner on his hands. The contract provision in question was a "may," not a "shall." The deadline date we claimed he had missed was merely a "target date." Big Bear Wally didn't do his homework. He didn't have a lesson plan. He didn't have a prepared agenda. He lost his composure, and he lost his control.

So you see, a little advanced planning, a careful check on your emotions, and a focus on simple and direct communications will help you realize that dismissal is a routine process that comes with the territory and not a dreadful nightmare that you hope and pray never comes your way.

CHAPTER 2

Insubordination Flows Too Freely

An In-Depth Examination of Insubordination and How to Eliminate It

Insubordination in its simplest terms means the refusal of an employee to follow a direct order. An order can come in the form of a directive, a policy, or even a verbal command. Obviously, a school can't operate if the teachers don't follow the principal's orders. Nor can any organization, including the military, succeed if this basic principle isn't honored.

My favorite story about insubordination comes by way of an old childhood friend of mine. He became a high-ranking officer in the U.S. Air Force, and he fired a subordinate officer for refusing to follow a direct order. In this case, it was a written policy that prohibited officers from engaging in extramarital affairs while in the service. One woman officer knew the policy but chose to ignore it. She got caught. She got fired.

Well, the proverbial crap hit the fan. Women's groups from all across the land were outraged. Sex discrimination, they cried. Politicians and civil libertarians took up the cause, and soon every newspaper in the country carried the banner headlines. She was being singled out merely because she was a woman. (This incident occurred prior to the Bill Clinton–Monica Lewinsky scandal, by the way.) My old buddy stood his ground, but he was under unbelievable pressure to reverse his decision.

It was a clear-cut issue to him. Insubordination cannot and will not be tolerated. The nature of the insubordinate act had nothing to do with it. The morality of marital infidelity wasn't the issue.

There was no question that the policy was clear and unambiguous. There was no question that the woman officer knew the policy and understood the policy. Her only claim was that she shouldn't have to honor such an outdated rule.

The commanding officer put it this way: "I can't have an officer flying multimillion-dollar F-15s loaded with nuclear bombs who refuses to follow an order when it doesn't suit her desires."

He was right. The heat subsided. He didn't get sidetracked. Insubordination in any form cannot be tolerated.

Oh, by the way, my old high school buddy—you might remember him: General Ronald Fogleman, chief of staff, U.S. Air Force, and the pilot was Kelly Flynn.

The old saying "You can't be a little bit pregnant" is a perfect analogy to being a little bit insubordinate. The fact is you can't be a little bit insubordinate, either. Either you are or you aren't. Administrators cannot tolerate insubordination, no matter how little the act seems, because it spreads like wildfire. One of the most basic tenets of labor relations holds that insubordination by an employee will not be permitted in the workplace. Even the unions hammer away at this concept because it is virtually impossible to win a case for an employee who commits an act of insubordination.

For some reason, however, many school administrators allow insubordinate acts to flow like beer at a political fund-raiser. Insubordination takes many forms, but refusal to follow an order or school policy is the most common.

Consider the case of Dorie, who was assigned to monitor students taking Maryland's assessment test. She bitterly opposed the test and did everything in her power to undermine its implementation. The principal assigned her to implement a checklist of items in her monitoring capacity. She blatantly refused and said she didn't care whether he wrote her up for insubordination.

Here was a textbook example of insubordination. Unbelievably, this principal did *not* write her up because he rationalized that it wasn't that big of a deal. Obviously, the word spread throughout the school, and the damaging precedent was engraved in granite.

In the private sector, this employee would have been fired on the spot, and there isn't an arbitrator in America who would have overturned the decision. Nor is there a union in the country that would have wasted money taking the case.

THERE'S NO LATITUDE FOR ATTITUDE

Let's take a look at another form of insubordination: the insubordinate act.

Candy was a disgruntled teacher who had been burned out for years. Her bitterness permeated her every word, action, and attitude. During one of her tirades in the principal's office, she became so agitated that she screamed, cursed, and stormed out of the office, slamming the door so hard it broke the window. Cursing out the boss, especially in the teaching profession, is in itself an act of insubordination that could easily justify dismissal. A competent administrator will never allow an employee to get away with such actions, as it will poison the entire staff. We all know incidents like this reach the other end of the school before the glass is picked up from the floor. Unfortunately, Candy never even received a verbal reprimand.

Don't ever allow this cancer to start in your school. Do not tolerate insubordination, no matter how minor you believe the issue to be. Once this cancer spreads, you will lose control of your school.

How much guff do you have to take? Too much, to be sure. But when the act reaches the level of insubordination and disrespect, you draw a line in the sand. If some kid in Candy's class would have committed a similar offense in her classroom, she would have demanded that the kid be strung up by his or her thumbs.

Principals have an obligation to make sure their directives are very clear and unambiguous. Make sure the teacher knows it is a directive, an order, and not merely a request. Be firm.

Don't confuse failure to follow a directive with refusal to obey. When a teacher fails to follow an order or neglects to get it done, it is not insubordination. This is neglect of duty, which of course is another valid and powerful cause for dismissal. Make sure, however, that you don't mix up the terms. If you confuse the terms, you will lose the case.

Likewise, a request of an employee is not a direct order; nor is the common practice of giving teachers advice on how to handle a situation. Sometimes administrators confuse these situations and charge insubordination, only to have it thrown back into their faces.

Danny was a middle school teacher who was much too friendly with the kids. He frequently took his students, male and female, on weekend outings, including dinner at his house. Even though his wife was always present, it opened him up to suspicion, and eventually he was accused by the parents of making improper comments to the girls he taught.

Before the parental complaints, the principal had cautioned Danny about his behavior with these words: "I'd advise you to be careful about bringing kids to your home. I don't think it's a good idea, and even though it's on your own time, I don't think you should do it." Once the allegations surfaced, the principal brought dismissal charges against Danny and cited him for insubordination. The principal rested his case on his prior statement, which he called a direct order.

This case illustrates perfectly the importance of making your direct order crystal-clear. Advice and admonishments and requests will not suffice. Danny was free to accept or reject his principal's advice without fear of being insubordinate. Being stupid is not synonymous with being insubordinate.

As a union representative, I was continually amazed at how much insubordination administrators allowed. Knowing that it is so difficult to win an appeal on such grounds, we were constantly educating our members about the dangers of insubordination. Actually, the union was often tougher on the teachers than the principals.

Every year the union would publish an article that I put together to emphasize to its member teachers the critical importance of this issue. It is printed at the end of this chapter so that principals and supervisors will realize how important it is to nip this cancer in the bud. It is a clear-cut winner for your side. So don't let it slip away.

INSUBORDINATION IN ITS MORE SUBTLE FORMS

Let's take a look at some activities that constitute insubordinate acts but that might not be so obvious.

Silence can be insubordination. You are having grade-level meetings to discuss ways to improve your assessment test scores. The fourth-grade team's members resent this activity and let you know it by their attitude and their actions. They just sit silently when you ask for input. They refuse to enter into any discussion despite your entreaties to open up the dialogue. If they do respond, it is negative and nonsupportive. They are thwarting cooperation by their obstinate attitude and their deliberate silence. This is clear-cut insubordination, even concerted job action, which is prohibited by law. It is a form of "slow down" or an on-the-job "strike," if you will.

If faced with this situation, you should clearly tell the grade-level participants that their input and their cooperation are required. If they persist in their silent treatment, you should cite every teacher for insubordination, in writing, and in their personnel files.

WORK NOW, GRIEVE LATER

I hope you know immediately what the above headline means, and you won't need to read any further. But don't take chances. If you're not . sure, or if you just don't know, read on. It may save your job someday.

The concept of "work now, grieve later" is one of the most basic rules in labor relations in America. Simply put, an employee must obey the order of an employer, even if it violates your contract. Refusal to obey a direct order is called *insubordination*, one of the five reasons for dismissal under the law.

But how can that be? Doesn't the contract guarantee my rights?

Fortunately, the answer is yes. But it is important that you follow the proper steps in seeking a remedy, if you're given a directive that you believe violates the negotiated agreement.

First, you should tell your principal or supervisor that you believe the directive is a violation of the agreement. This may result in the order being withdrawn or modified. If the principal persists, you must comply with the order, and then file a grievance. The grievance procedure will correct the problem. Doing it the other way around can result in the classic case of "winning the battle and losing the war."

Courts have consistently upheld the firing of an employee when he or she refused to follow an order . . . even when it was found to be in direct violation of the contract. An employee has the right to refuse an order if it is immoral, illegal, or places his or her life in jeopardy.

Of course there is a difference between a "direct order" from an employer and a "request." If your principal is merely asking you to do something that violates the teacher's contract, you have a right to say no.

A word of caution: Before you refuse, make absolutely certain that the principal is requesting and not directing.

CHAPTER 3

School Reform's Greatest Obstacle

How Deadwood in the Classroom Stands in the Way

No Child Left Behind. Assessment tests. Principals getting demoted and fired because of poor test scores. These are the present-day realities. School reform is here to stay, and whether you agree or not, you're being judged by the student's scores.

Nine principals in Prince Georges County, Maryland, home of the Redskins and Andrews Air Force Base, were demoted just two days before the opening of school this year. Reason: poor scores on assessment tests.

It stands to reason that your students' test scores aren't going to improve if you have a handful of incompetent teachers on your faculty. Poor teachers who can only bring you down are what I call *deadwood*.

Can these assessment tests really bring about public school reform? Will the kids' test scores improve and their schools reach a successful level of achievement? Will the public hail the new era as the salvation of our public schools?

. Will we reach the hyperbolic level proclaimed by Al Gore that most public schools are excellent?

The answer is no.

It is impossible to achieve true school reform until we dump the deadwood from every public school building in the United States. We simply cannot wave a magic wand and make our schools better. We must remove the element that is causing the decline in the first place. Until we bite this bullet, all of our fancy programs and pronouncements end up in the wastebasket marked failure!

But what about the kids? Many of us graduated from college believing in the ideals of the teaching profession, optimistic that we could change society by being the best teachers in the school. We believed that the future depended on the high quality of education we were about to impart. Idealistic. Optimistic. Enthusiastic. Dedicated. Good people who would do a good job.

It didn't take long for us to learn a terrible truth. There was an element, one or two of our colleagues, who had long since lost that luster. Bitching had replaced brilliance. *Burnout* was the word of the day. The cynicism that often permeated the faculty room was as thick as the smoke from teachers' cigarettes. A sad reality struck home: They just didn't care. It became apparent that the quality of their teaching was a mirror image of their performance in the classroom.

A favorite graduate school professor once startled our class by proclaiming that every one of us knew the good teachers in our school without ever setting foot in their classrooms. As time went on, we soon learned that his point was well taken. Even those of you who are denying it as you read these words know in your heart of hearts that the professor was right. By the same token, we all knew the deadwood, too. And year after year they came back—and the rotting of our public schools kept creeping slowly but surely into every school building in the country.

After thirty-two years, this reality hasn't changed much. The cynicism continues. The bitching still permeates far too many faculty rooms. In fact, the only real change in the faculty room atmosphere is the clean air brought on by the "no smoking" laws.

The stench of deadwood is still there. And the sad fact is that far too many of us have stood idly by and allowed the deadwood to remain. I myself certainly admit to contributing far too much to this continuance in the performance of my duties with the Maryland State Teachers Association and the Delaware State Education Association.

Unfortunately, the public caught on, too. Instead of admiring teachers, many people feel contempt for them in far too many locales.

The very essence of public education as we've known it over the years is at risk. Witness the National Education Association (NEA) and the American Federation of Teachers (AFT)—longtime bitter rivals— on the verge of merger. The number one issue driving the consolidation is their joint crusade to save public education. (Some say the merger talks are motivated by the altruistic desire to save the schools. Others believe it is their overwhelming desire to survive.) But no one denies that the driving force is the recognition that our schools are in trouble.

School reform! The politicians, the public, the press, everybody is on board with this message. Even the unions have realized that the only way to reverse this downward spiral is to embrace school reform. More and more of these segments of society are recognizing the only real reform of our schools is the removal of the teachers who aren't carrying their weight.

Look at the NEA. It has endorsed what it calls the "new unionism." The centerpiece of this movement is its much-heralded "Peer Assistance and Review Program." The NEA says it will help school systems rid themselves of incompetent teachers via a joint effort to "counsel the participating teacher out of the profession." Now you know if the unions are openly advocating a process to police their own ranks, the problem is more fact than fiction.

Administrators have a moral, as well as professional, obligation to weed out the deadwood. They also have a mandate to curb the growing number of mediocre teachers in our classrooms. The public demands excellence. We can't have world-class schools without world-class teachers. Mediocrity and deadwood in the teaching profession are the two greatest threats to the public schools in America today. If administrators don't stop this, who will?

You know, the most unfortunate part of this entire scenario is the shadow it casts on the truly outstanding teachers who are busting their butts every day to provide quality education for our kids. We are all reduced to the lowest common denominator when the debate rages on. We're only as strong as our weakest link.

People don't cite the excellent teacher when they criticize the school system. They cite the deadwood. They quote the mediocre teachers who themselves bad-mouth the system every chance they get. You see, the malcontents are hurting all of us by their dissatisfaction, and not just in the classroom. They hurt the good teachers. They hurt the good administrators. They hurt the public schools as an institution. And, worst of all, they hurt the kids!

With three decades of firsthand experience as a teacher advocate, I discovered how desperately administrators need training in dismissal skills. We cannot expect principals and supervisors to get rid of the deadwood and the mediocrity if we don't give them the professional support to do the job.

The same spirit that motivated a young college grad many years ago drives the development of *Dismissal Doesn't Have to Be Difficult* today: a belief that the public school system is the most valuable experiment in the short history of democracy in America, a belief that the future of our country rests in the hands of those who supervise and evaluate our teachers, and a knowledge that we cannot allow our society to be shaped by anything less than excellence in the classroom.

Brooks Adams (1838–1918) said it best: "A teacher affects eternity. You can never tell when the influence stops." Remember this: The sword cuts both ways, so a bad teacher can have a lasting effect, too.

The mission of *Dismissal Doesn't Have to Be Difficult* is to give principals and supervisors the skills and knowledge needed to guarantee that our kids will never again be influenced by mediocrity or, God forbid, the stench of deadwood!

CHAPTER 4

Ignoring the Weapons You Have

Overlooked Opportunities to Act

What if you could wave a magic wand and make tenure disappear? That would solve your dismissal problems, wouldn't it? All schools would be free from mediocre, marginal, and incompetent teachers. Wow!

Not so fast. Let's take a reality check. In my many years of experience, I found that principals, supervisors, and superintendents far too often don't even use the weapons they have.

Let's take a look at the state of Maryland, for example, and its challenge-free disciplinary procedure: the second-class certificate.

The greatest weapon never used by administrators is the second-class certificate.

It's been on the books since the 1930s in Maryland, and the dust on its covers is so thick that school administrators must not be able to find it on the shelf. Union folks have been perplexed by this phenomenon for years. If only principals and supervisors realized how easy it is to use, it would become a staple in the field of teacher accountability.

Do you realize that the Maryland State Teachers Association has never won an appeal of a second-class certificate case? And guess what? It never will! It is your most protected course of action—use it!

Believe it or not, every teacher is automatically placed on a second-class status at the time of employment, and the superintendent must make a judgment at the end of two years to change second class to first class. After that, a new judgment must be made every two years to maintain first-class status. The law says that being placed on first-class is not automatic. It requires affirmative action (with a small *a*) to rate a teacher other than second class.

Truth be told, it just doesn't happen this way. Our system has ignored this law for decades. You are probably doubting my assertion at this very moment. Go ahead, get a law book and see for yourself. Our practices pretend that you must take action to reduce a teacher from first class to second, when in fact the law mandates exactly the opposite. Can you believe it? We snatch defeat from the jaws of victory.

Before reading on, name the four standards for classification. What are the legal reasons to justify placing a teacher on second-class certification status? By the way, did you know that the administration is mandated to consider each of these reasons before rating a teacher first class? It is a "shall," not a "may," in the law. Here they are, right from Section 6-103 of the Maryland Code:

- Scholarship
- Executive ability
- Personality
- Teaching efficiency

When is the last time you seriously and specifically considered these four legally mandated criteria when you wrote your evaluation report for a teacher?

The Maryland State Board of Education has never reversed a second-class certificate decision, and thus the courts have never even considered trying to reverse the state. Using this course of action to deal with your mediocre teachers and your deadwood should be a no-brainer. Second-class certificates are a godsend for administrators about to begin the dismissal process for a tenured teacher. Although not required or even contemplated by state law or legal precedence, it is a good way to ease into the dismissal mode. It can be particularly comforting for those of you who really hate the idea of being thought of as unfair. You place a teacher on second class, give him or her a few months or a year to improve, and if he or she doesn't, you dismiss this teacher without a tinge of guilt.

This strategy is also effective for the good teacher who has turned sour for whatever reason. Experience shows that teachers in this category often get a shock to their system from being placed on second class, snap out of it, and return to first class with renewed vigor and excellence. One such teacher described his demotion to second class as "a professional kick in the ass," and for him it worked. It also can spur the mediocre teacher to take the steps necessary to grow professionally and to enter the realm of excellence.

There is an economic penalty attached to second-class status, as the teacher's salary is frozen at its current level. In many cases, the teacher loses as much as $1,000 or $2,000. Clearly, the action delivers a chilling message. We realize that second-class decisions, like all dismissal-related decisions, are technically made by the superintendent. But the reality is that the rubber meets the road at your office door.

"But I don't work in Maryland, so what's the big deal?" I can see your brain waves right now. I can hear your indignant questions, too. Just because the administrators in Maryland don't act doesn't mean we sleep on our rights out here. Let's take a closer look.

It has been my observation that too many administrators bestow the cloak of tenure protection on everyone on the staff: custodians, secretaries, nurses, teacher's aides, you name it. The dread of dismissal and the unnecessary fear of a union challenge permeate far too many administrative offices. Think back to the last time you fired an employee. Mattie's story illustrates my point.

MATTIE

Mattie was a teacher's aide in a suburban elementary school. Her poor performance was outdone only by her lousy attitude and disruptive behavior. None of the teachers wanted her assigned to their classroom. She was the classic "heater" spewing distrust and discontent throughout the entire school. She somehow managed to get into everybody's business. I don't think she had a friend on the entire staff. She objected to playground duty, especially when it was cold out. When the temperature dipped, she called in sick. She refused to help the classroom teachers clean up their room after a student accident, and she objected to clerical duties even though they were an integral part of her job description. She was the schoolhouse gossip. She was a habitual bitcher.

By the way, this was a nonunion environment. Support personnel had no collective bargaining rights, no contract, and no grievance procedure. The courts had ruled that they were not entitled to an appeal beyond the superintendent level.

Mattie's previous principal had evaluated her unsatisfactory. The current principal gave her an unsatisfactory evaluation as well. Several teachers signed a letter of complaint about the way she mistreated the kids. She was mean with them. Fed up with all of this, the principal recommended dismissal.

Before long, the assistant superintendent showed up with a message of caution. "Are you sure we have a paper trail?" he inquired. The principal's inch-thick file put that question to rest. "But you know she will fight this!" the assistant superintendent continued. The gutsy principal pushed on: "I want her out of this school, and so do the teachers." The recommendation went on to the superintendent's desk, without comment from his assistant. His reaction was worse. "We will really look bad if this gets out," he admonished. He bobbed and weaved like Muhammad Ali in the Thrilla at Manila as the principal pushed for dismissal. "The board has to give her a hearing, you know," he concluded erroneously.

Treating this nontenured, nonunionized, noncertified aide with the kid gloves of a tenured teacher, the superintendent refused to fire Mattie. Instead, he put her back in the same school for another try the next year.

This classic mistake is made over and over again. Don't ever allow such a precedent in your school or district. Never bestow the protection of tenure on those who aren't entitled.

CHAPTER 5

Kids Make the Tough Calls Easy

One Simple Question Makes Hard Evaluation Decisions Easy

To hear the experts talk, you'd think it takes a Ph.D. to understand the nuances of teacher evaluation. Professional journals pontificate about the theoretical aspects of evaluation. They throw around words like *summative evaluation* and *formative evaluation*, and folks in education circles just smile and pretend they know what it all means.

Take a look at this gem, for example. It is a compilation of quotes from various professional journals that I have pieced together to illustrate my point. While it is not an exact quote, it does not invent a single phrase:

> Concepts like professional growth within the context of local educational institutions as professional learning communities must be promulgated system-wide as a deviation from the norm of our culture of isolation in the classroom.

Maybe you understand this kind of jargon. Frankly, I don't get it. In teacher evaluation, the most important factor is to make sure it is easily understood by the people being evaluated as well as the people doing the evaluation. It must be clear, simple, and concise. Relying on fancy words with lots of syllables is the wrong way to go in this field. It reminds me of the collective bargaining contracts that are written by lawyers. They sound like a Supreme Court pleading, and the only people who understand the language are the lawyers for the board and the union. Of course, good contracts, like good evaluation language, are written in plain speaking terms so that the average Joe and Jane in the classroom can figure out what they're supposed to do.

Sometimes I think educators create their pedagogical lexicon to confuse everybody so as to guarantee their own job security. If they are the only ones who know what they're talking about, we have to keep them around to bring us up to speed.

Good evaluation theory doesn't have to be difficult at all. In fact, you only need a one-syllable word to figure it out. All you need to do is focus on what I call the "magic question."

The single word is *kids*. Keep your eye on the sparrow, folks. Remember why we are all here in the first place. Don't get bogged down in extraneous considerations. In the end they don't really matter.

If you begin every observation or evaluation decision with one simple question, you will relieve 99 percent of the stress you feel when dealing with this issue. If it is a close call, you will find this magic question makes the choice obvious.

Simply ask yourself, "Would I want my own son or daughter exposed to this teacher?"

It's that simple, really. Each of us wants a world-class education for our own kids. We want excellence in the classroom, not mediocrity for our sons and daughters. And so it should be for every kid in our schools.

We must raise the bar on our expectations of teaching performance. We should expect excellence, not just satisfactory teaching. That's what we look for when we observe a teacher. That's what we want in every classroom, every day!

Don't be tempted to take a powder when it comes to making that tough call. I've seen principals who take the easy way out rather than face the hassle of dealing with an unsatisfactory observation or evaluation situation. Unfortunately, this happens far too frequently. And this option will always come back to haunt you sometime in the future when you finally decide to take action to rid your school of the mediocre performer.

Remember when you were a teacher? Remember how good it felt to help a kid and to see that sparkle in the child's eye when you knew you had connected? Remember the thrill of that teachable moment? Since becoming an administrator, you may have found that those special rewards are few and far between. But your commitment to the kids is still as strong as ever, and you have to find new venues to demonstrate that belief.

Dedicating your career to the principle outlined in this chapter is the most powerful way you can realize this ideal. From this day forth and forevermore, pledge to ask that simple question every time you make a judgment call about the teachers' performance. "Would I want my own son or daughter exposed to this teacher?"

CHAPTER 6

Dismiss a Teacher: Five Easy Calls

Dismissible Behaviors That Can't Be Overturned

It really is not impossible or even very difficult to weed out the dead-wood. Often the evidence is right in front of your face, but you don't recognize it. Some behaviors are so egregious that dismissal is justified by the act alone. There are at least five situations that make dismissal a piece of cake.

1. LATENESS

Can you tolerate a teacher who habitually comes to work late? Should you? What if he or she is a good teacher otherwise?

Believe it or not, tardiness is almost never tolerated in the workplace of America when the case ends up in court or before an arbitrator. Dismissals are always upheld in these legal reviews unless a very, very compelling set of circumstances warrants a reversal. In fact, I cannot think of a single example of a reversal in my thirty-two years of experience.

The basic labor relations principle goes back to the private sector model. You can't run the assembly line if one of the workers isn't there, and thus production is shut down because of one worker's tardiness.

Does this really apply to a school setting? You bet it does. We can't have twenty-five kids sitting in a classroom without a teacher there to supervise. We can't have that early-morning Admission, Review, and Dismissal meeting if the classroom teacher isn't there. You get the picture.

Of course, there's more to it than the direct effect of that one teacher's work requirements. Lateness by one employee affects the entire workforce. First, it creates inconvenience for the other workers.

Second, it triggers resentment in other staff members. (If I have to come to work on time, why shouldn't you?) Third, it creates morale problems in your school. By allowing one teacher to slide, you create the atmosphere that telegraphs to the entire staff that punctuality isn't a job requirement. Far too many principals are lax on this issue. Just looking the other way is a common practice in many schools, especially if the person is a good teacher in the classroom. And if you create the past practice of not enforcing it with the "good" teacher, you make it impossible to enforce it with the deadwood. Therefore, the enforcement of punctuality must be even-handed for the entire faculty.

Keep in mind that we're not talking about the occasional flat tire or the failed alarm clock. We all run into those situations, and they are to be overlooked. It's the habitual lateness, the clear and consistent pattern of tardiness, that we are addressing. Later we will deal with how to document this lateness and how to actually follow through with a dismissal recommendation.

2. FAILURE OR REFUSAL TO REPORT CHILD ABUSE

No room for compromise here. If a teacher fails to file a suspected case of child abuse, dismissal may very well be in order. In Maryland, this cause of action is specifically written into the law, so you would clearly be protected and upheld if you brought this action. Now there may be circumstances that could justify a teacher's failure to file the report, but they would have to be extraordinary for you to look the other way. Keep in mind, you are liable for this failure, too.

A teacher's refusal to file can never be tolerated. We advise you to recommend dismissal in writing if you have a teacher who will not file the report. Based on our experience, this refusal can take some interesting twists and turns.

The case of Corby comes to mind. She did not want to file a child abuse report because she knew the parents and didn't want to get involved. She advised the guidance counselor of the suspected abuse, who in turn advised the principal. The counselor filed the necessary report with Social Services, but the teacher did not. Under Maryland law, at that time, a teacher was required to file a report even if he or she knew another staff member had already filed. The teacher had an option of jointly filing with the counselor, but she did not have the option of ignoring it.

When approached by the principal about her reluctance to file the report, Corby confirmed her refusal. The principal explained the law and her option of a joint filing, advising Corby that her actions could place her job in jeopardy. So Corby changed her story. She stated, "Well, then, I will just say that I didn't suspect child abuse." This principal could have brought dismissal charges on this incident alone. The union could not have won an appeal. In fact, it never would have taken the case.

Did the principal take any action against Corby? Don't ask. You really don't want to hear the answer.

3. VIOLATION OF CONFIDENTIALITY

If a teacher violates the confidentiality of information he or she has obtained in the course of employment, dismissal is warranted. This behavior can take many different forms, of course. Here are some of the classic examples I have seen:

- Revealing the name of the person who filed child abuse charges
- Sharing reassignment decisions made by the principal but not ready for publication
- Disclosing disciplinary actions taken against another teacher
- Sharing private information about a parent's lifestyle
- Pumping the secretary for confidential information

Each of these violations of confidentiality would have been sufficient grounds for dismissal.

4. SEXUAL HARASSMENT IN THE WORKPLACE

Zero tolerance is the only standard allowable here. It is your obligation to guarantee a nonhostile work environment with regard to sexual harassment. You are responsible, and you will be held accountable if someone brings charges.

Faculty members' levels of tolerance may run the gamut from innocent and naive to wild and woolly. You can't take any chances. What's an innocent comment to one can be highly offensive to someone else. It may even change from day to day with each individual. We've seen it time and again. A principal explains that he has joked with the female teacher many times and she has joked with him. Then all of a sudden she accuses him of sexual harassment for the very thing they've been doing all year. (We've seen it the other way around with female principals and male teachers, too.)

Believe me, when you see those innocent comments in writing, perhaps out of context, they are stark and harsh, and they look devastating on an Equal Employment Opportunity Commission form.

Jokes with a sexual message or overtone are like sticks of dynamite just waiting to explode in your faculty room. This is by far the most prevalent example of sexual harassment in our workplace today. If one member of your faculty finds these jokes offensive, a hostile work environment exists. Obviously, the principal can control his or her own joke telling. Just stop doing it.

But what about the teacher-to-teacher jokes that may be commonplace in and around the school? How can you be held accountable for the actions of others? Bottom line: you are!

It's impossible to stop the joke telling completely; in fact, you really don't want to. After all, we want good staff morale, and humor is an essential element of that atmosphere. This is a very delicate balancing act to pull off. Jokes and levity, yes. Jokes with a sexual innuendo, no.

Your obligation is to communicate the zero-tolerance policy to the faculty in a clear and concise manner. Then you enforce the policy without exception. Obviously, there are many other forms of sexual harassment, and this zero tolerance applies to all of them.

5. ETHNIC SLURS, LYING, STEALING, CHEATING, AND ILLEGAL ACTS

Zero tolerance is obvious here, too, right? Not so. Unfortunately I could fill a page or two with examples of teachers who remain on duty today despite having committed these blatant offenses. Dismissal is so easy here that there is just no excuse for these offenses to continue. Let me share the most egregious example I ever witnessed during my years as a UniServ director.

Marion

Marion was a media specialist in a small-town high school. She was tenured and had worked in the school for fifteen years, but, for the most part, her work was less than satisfactory. Teachers complained about her performance. Students complained about her poor attitude, and even the parents complained about the way she treated their kids. She seemed particularly insensitive when dealing with minority students. She had received more than a few "needs improvements" on her evaluation from the administration. You might say she was one of those "frequent fliers" who spent a good bit of time in the union office. We could have filled the pages of a book with the number of rebuttals she wrote over the years.

Her principal made it quite clear that he wanted her out of the school, and he was just waiting for the green light from the central office to take the action necessary to achieve his goal. Knowing this background will help you understand my perplexed reaction when he passed up his golden opportunity.

Marion was sipping coffee one morning in the faculty room and chatting with one of her colleagues. Just outside the door a group of African American kids were fooling around and making far too much noise in the hall. As the noise grew louder, Marion grew more and more frustrated, as it was disrupting the peace and quiet of her planning period. She vented her anger by throwing up her arms and spewing out, "Look at those [n-word] out there."

The startled look on her colleague's face was matched only by the angry shouts of another teacher who was resting on the sofa. Marion hadn't noticed that there was another person in the room—an African American history teacher. She immediately began to apologize profusely, but, of course, to no avail. He went straight to the principal's office, and Marion ran to the phone to call the union.

I told Marion to expect dismissal charges. I also told her that she had no chance of winning, so she might as well begin preparing herself for the inevitability of resignation. I explained that in accordance with state law, she would receive the notification via certified mail within ten days following the conference with her principal, which I was sure would be held within the hour. I was particularly certain that she would be fired in light of a similar incident, in the same district, whereby a school board member was forced to resign when he let loose an ethnic slur.

The principal was furious, and he met with Marion before the day was over. He gave her a severe tongue lashing, ordered her to apologize, in writing, to the teachers who had witnessed the incident, and he placed a scathing letter of reprimand in her personnel file.

But that was it. No suspension. No dismissal. And, to this day, I can't figure out why!

Dismissal was fully justified, probably even mandatory under the circumstances. I'm virtually certain the association would never have appealed this case even if Marion had been Teacher of the Year. Here was a clear-cut winner for the principal. It was a once-in-a-lifetime opportunity to dump some deadwood without a ripple of dissention. It was the easiest of the Five Easy Calls, but the school district let it slip right out of its hands.

CHAPTER 7

Documentation

The Key to Success

I used to throw around an expression that puts this chapter into proper perspective: "If it ain't in writing, it don't exist." Believe me, this poor grammar captures the heart and soul of any dismissal action. To win, you must be able to show a paper trail. Even in cases dealing with the egregious issues of chapter 6, you must have written documentation to sustain a dismissal action. You need to be very careful, however, about what you write and how you write it. *Dismissal Doesn't Have to Be Difficult* will show you the many pitfalls to avoid—the ones the union will exploit if you don't.

DOCUMENT, DOCUMENT, DOCUMENT

If you don't comprehend anything else from this book, this is the chapter to remember. Without good documentation, you have nothing. With thorough documentation, you can't lose. Documentation is merely writing down an anecdotal record of what occurred. Date it, time it, and accurately record the facts as well as the flavor. Capture the event as specifically as you possibly can and write it in a timely fashion.

While you shouldn't put it off until the next day, you should never write it in a fit of anger. Give yourself a little bit of time to cool down before you pick up the pen. You can't trust your memory, so you want to write it while the facts are fresh. Be sure to include the names of the people involved, as well as their relevant comments. Do not allow ambiguity to enter into your written page.

Shakespeare said, "Brevity is the soul of wit." I say, "Anything over one page is a waste of paper." In both cases the message is clear. Get to the point. State the obvious, and call the shots the way you see them.

THE MORE YOU WRITE, THE MORE THEY FIGHT

Lengthy narratives were the boon of this union representative's existence. I used to love them. The more you write, the more ammunition you give the union.

For example, we always looked for inconsistencies within the narrative itself.

Often, there were subtle contradictions. We also looked for spelling errors, grammatical errors, and other comments that could be used to make the administrator look less than professional. Keep in mind that your documentation may very well be read by your boss, the board, the union, a judge, and maybe your neighbors if it becomes a public issue. You never know.

Administrators tend to shy away from graphic descriptive words, especially if they are negative. This is a mistake. If it is OK for the Ten Commandments to be stated in negative terms, it's OK for a principal to use them, too. Remember, be clear; be concise; use simple language; use simple sentences.

By the way, I recommend that you write a rough draft. Have it typed by your confidential secretary, wait two hours, and then reread it before deciding whether to sign it. Discretion is the better part of valor.

What is the correct order for writing your documentation? I strongly recommend that you go to the heart of the case first. State what you are recommending as a cause of action, then follow it with your supporting facts. Communicate the problem immediately. If the teacher's action represents misconduct in office, state it up front. Otherwise, you run the risk of the teacher missing the point or failing to recognize the severity of the issue. You also run the risk of your superintendent arriving at a lesser course of action if he or she doesn't grasp your resolve right at the beginning. This sequence helps build support from your superintendent because he or she realizes you mean business right from the get-go.

How do you document continuing problems, such as lateness, to establish a pattern? Easy. Keep track of these incidents in a notebook, a file in your desk drawer, or even on your schedule book. Make sure these are kept in places that guarantee confidentiality. This is critical. Just jot down the dates and times for each occurrence. When you are sure that a pattern exists, you can use this documentation to proceed with an appropriate disciplinary course of action. Contemporaneous notes are very powerful pieces of evidence in any hearing.

Often I am asked if you have to show these files to the teacher. The answer is quite simple: Why not? If the teacher asks to see them, go ahead. It is always better to err on the side of openness and fairness. Furthermore, we're not advocating a CIA operation—merely a record of the infractions, which the teacher already knows he or she has committed. On the other hand, check your local union agreement to see if this issue is addressed. No need to go overboard if the union has agreed to something less than I have suggested.

Scripting, as it was used in the districts I represented, can be one of the greatest things since sliced bread for a union representative. The supervisor or principal would script the entire lesson and then include the script in the observation report presented to the teacher. The field is fertile for misspelled words, improper grammar, lack of punctuation, failure to capitalize, poor sentence structure, not to mention terrible penmanship. If you use scripting in the way I experienced it, and if you are given a choice, should you use it? No way—it's a gimme for the union.

One of my favorite tricks was to hire an English professor from a local college or university to grade the script. If it was loaded with grammatical errors, I had the professor testify at the dismissal hearing. This tactic was especially effective at a public hearing. I can recall one case in which the teacher was being dismissed for incompetence, and a part of their documentation was her inability to use proper grammar. Our local professor had graded the script of one of the supervisors, and it was loaded with spelling errors and improper tense usage. The supervisor got an F on her script and her other notes. Fortunately for the school district, the teacher resigned, and we never got the opportunity to put that professor on the witness stand. The local television stations were primed to show up for the public hearing that night.

CHAPTER 8

Consistency Is Critical

Inconsistency Is the Union's Best Friend

Ralph Waldo Emerson once said, "A foolish consistency is the hobgoblin of little minds." Well, he sure wasn't talking about the dismissal of teachers. Inconsistency is a cornerstone of the union's defense strategy.

Did you write up one teacher for being late and only verbally warn another? Did you suspend a male teacher for telling an off-color joke while only writing a letter of reprimand for the female teacher who did the same thing? Competent union representatives will scour every document in existence to find these inconsistencies. Sometimes they are right in front of their eyes.

The most frequent discovery of inconsistency comes from comparing the write-ups of the principal with those of the supervisor or vice principal. You might be surprised to learn that often the union finds inconsistencies within your own writings and actions.

MOLLY

Molly, a twenty-one-year veteran teacher, was late for school every single day. She was mediocre minus in the classroom. Discussions between the principal and vice principal centered around placing her on a second-class certificate. The supervisors agreed that she was "burnout" personified. Her classes were boring. She didn't display one ounce of enthusiasm, and she did nothing to prepare her kids for Maryland's assessment test. Oh, yeah, she also taught third grade—a testing grade in Maryland.

When the principal finally conferenced with Molly about her tardiness, she responded plaintively by asking, "Well, just what time am I supposed to be at school?" By the way, this conference was held only after several teachers complained about the unfairness of her lateness.

Now for the rest of the story. Think she was placed on second-class certification? Think she received an unsatisfactory evaluation? Guess again. Magic Molly was nominated by this principal to be Teacher of the Year!

It is critical that the left hand know what the right hand is doing. Having documentation from more than one administrative source is very powerful evidence and should be used whenever possible. Just be aware of the pitfalls if reports from different sources aren't consistent.

EILEEN

Eileen was the principal of a large elementary school in a rural section of the county. She knew one of her third-year teachers was a problem. The other teachers in her wing of the school had lodged complaints about her lackadaisical performance. Teaching a testing grade in Maryland, the other teachers were worried that this young lady would bring down their scores.

Eileen intensified her observation schedule and discovered that this teacher needed to improve or else. She discussed her findings with the assistant principal, and they began a concerted effort to achieve her goal. During the next three months, they had documented her poor performance with at least three unsatisfactory observations.

Believing this teacher's poor performance would speak for itself, Eileen never felt the need to inform the supervisor of elementary education about her plan of action. The supervisor worked out of the central office, so coordination with her was more difficult than with the school's assistant principal.

Before long, the supervisor paid a classroom visit to the teacher in question. The lesson was an unmitigated disaster. She rated the observation unsatisfactory. Seems like Eileen's game plan is right on track, right? Wrong—the supervisor was a kind-hearted soul, and when the teacher pleaded for another chance, she agreed. Another observation was scheduled, and this time the lesson went fairly well; the supervisor rated it satisfactory. She destroyed the unsatisfactory report and placed the satisfactory one in the teacher's file.

Eileen, the well-intentioned principal, committed the cardinal sin. She failed to coordinate her strategy with the full management team, and as a result, a major inconsistency in the stream of evidence entered the files. Had the supervisor known about Eileen's plan of action, she would never have agreed to give the teacher a second chance. Needless to say, we pounced on this inconsistency in our appeal meeting with the principal, and she was forced to put off her disciplinary actions for another day.

WILL YOUR ACTIONS STAND THE TEST WHEN CHALLENGED?

Dr. Wayne W. Dyer's admonition to "banish doubt and carry it out" comes into play here. I prefer to put it a little less delicately: "When in doubt, dump 'em." The point is, doubt and foreboding are greater enemies than all of the unions in the world. When doubt creeps into your mind, remember the question in chapter 5: "Would I want my own son or daughter exposed to this teacher?"

To help evaluate your actions, I am including the standards that the unions apply to measure your actions. Does your decision meet the test of "just cause" as defined in the field of labor relations? I believe arbitrator Carroll R. Daugherty's seven tests for just cause represent the best description available:

- Did the employer give the employee forewarning or foreknowledge of the possible or probable disciplinary consequences of the employee's conduct?
- Was the employer's rule or managerial order reasonably related to the orderly, efficient, and safe operation of the employer's business?
- Did the employer, before administering discipline to an employee, make an effort to discover whether the employee did in fact violate or disobey a rule or order of management?
- Was the employer's investigation conducted fairly and objectively?

- At the investigation, did the "judge" obtain substantial evidence or proof that the employee was guilty as charged?
- Has the employer applied its rules, orders, and penalties to all employees in an even-handed manner and without discrimination?
- Was the degree of discipline administered by the employer in a particular case reasonably related to (1) the seriousness of the employee's proven offense and (2) the record of the employee in his or her service with the employer?

According to Daugherty, a no answer to one or more of these questions normally signifies that just cause did not exist. In other words, a no means that the employer's disciplinary decision contained one or more elements of arbitrary, capricious, unreasonable, and/or discriminatory action to such an extent that the arbitrator would rule against the employer.

Daugherty's seven tests have been covered in so many union training sessions over the years that they are pretty much accepted as the "gospel" in preparing for a teacher case. Knowing what the union reps are looking for will help you avoid their traps.

CHAPTER 9

Time Limits and Deadline Dates

Why You Can't Afford to Let Them Slide

Missed time limits or deadline dates accounted for a majority of the victories I enjoyed as a union representative. It is the first thing the unions check. Time limits and deadline dates must be met by both parties in labor relations. To adhere to them, you have to know what they are.

So, first and foremost, my advice is to study the contract, the board policy manual, the administrative procedures manual, your building policy book, and all of the relevant state laws. Simply put, you must know these time limits and deadline dates by heart. The union will know them for sure. Arbitrators and courts will not allow you to prevail in a dismissal action, regardless of the quality of your documentation, if you miss the time limit or fail to meet a deadline.

Furthermore, if you do not follow the deadline dates in the various policy documents, the union will win a reversal of whatever action you have taken. In fact, virtually all of the successful evaluation-related cases won by the unions are won because of these technicalities. They seldom win evaluation-type cases on the merits.

Never assume that your superiors know these dates—this advice includes your superintendent. It is your responsibility to know the deadlines and to make sure you haven't missed any in the process.

What should you do if you fail to meet a deadline date in the completion of an observation or evaluation report? Don't ever try to back-date it or otherwise attempt to cover up your mistake. Accept it and suck it up.

NANCY JANE AND MRS. CHAPEL

Nancy Jane was an experienced teacher, having taught about fifteen years in three different school systems. This was her third time to gain tenure, so she was well aware of the state guidelines and timetables.

She was perplexed because her end-of-the-year observation report and subsequent conference had not yet been scheduled. Mrs. Chapel, the supervisor, had visited Nancy's classroom and had done the observation. The deadline date for receiving the written observation report and follow-up conference, however, was the previous Friday.

That afternoon, Mrs. Chapel popped into Nancy's classroom all bright and cheery with a file folder in hand. After a pleasant "Hi and how are you," this supervisor handed Nancy a copy of her back-dated observation report with a pen and said, "Here, sign this. It will be OK since everything was satisfactory. We do this all the time." In all of her fifteen years, Nancy had never seen anything like this. Having been through the nontenure routine two times before in two different school systems, she knew this was a strange and inappropriate request. But she was perplexed and felt a tremendous amount of pressure to go along with her superior. After all, this was the person who was going to determine whether or not she got tenure.

Nancy Jane, however, was no rookie. She had gained tenure in two other Maryland school systems, she had been through a strike in her first year of teaching, she had been rated excellent by two other schools, she had done in-service training on the teaching of reading for one county, and she had heard hundreds of hours of lectures about teachers' rights at the dinner table for the past thirty years.

Nancy Jane put on her red-framed glasses, shot a look of disdain at Mrs. Chapel, and handed back the pen. The supervisor was stunned. This had never happened before. She got the message from the intense nonverbal communication and said, "Er, uh, OK then," and walked out the door. Nothing further was ever said about this incident, and Nancy Jane achieved tenure for the third time in her career.

You don't have to be a rocket scientist to realize that Mrs. Chapel's actions were inappropriate and unprofessional. In reality, her actions were illegal. Don't ever think of asking a teacher to cover up for you if you miss a deadline. Mrs. Chapel could have been fired for her misconduct in office.

Just like in love and war, timing is a critical ingredient in your dismissal strategy.

It is important to notify the teacher of any perceived problem as soon as you observe it. You must allow ample time for the teacher to make the adjustments necessary to correct the problem.

In addition, you need to allow yourself ample time to provide recommendations for improvement and professional assistance in order to help the teacher meet those goals.

One of the basic strategies of the union will be to question whether the administration offered appropriate suggestions for improvement, as well as ample time for the teacher to implement these suggestions. While they will argue that you didn't meet these requirements no matter what you do, following the advice offered here will guarantee you a win on this issue.

By the way, this tip is a double-edged sword. The teacher and the union must meet their deadlines and time limits, too. Never make an exception with regard to deadlines for evaluation-related requirements. If you make an exception for one teacher, you will be forced to make an exception for others or face charges of bias or harassment.

If you snooze, you lose. If they snooze, they lose.

CHAPTER 10

Personality Conflicts

Do You Have to Put Up with Them?

"We just have a personality conflict, that's all." You've heard that remark a dozen times, and that's supposed to be the end of the story. Somehow principals are expected to put up with this aggravation day after day. Most of you have been led to believe that you're stuck with the "heaters" on your staff. (*Heater* is an old sports term that describes a player who always keeps things stirred up on the team and causes dissention.) Most faculties have at least one, and that person manages to poison the atmosphere for the entire staff. You can bet that staff morale is damaged by the influence of a "negaholic."

The truth is you don't have to tolerate such behavior. Believe it or not, you can fire a teacher like this and fully justify it under the incompetence term. Courts have held that personality problems, composure problems, judgment problems, and attitude problems fit squarely under the incompetence label. You see, a competent teacher will modify his or her personality to accommodate cooperation with the rest of the faculty and administration. The same is true of any employee whether he or she is in the school system or out there working on construction. Disharmony in the workplace is not a constitutionally protected activity.

School administrators need to make this expectation clear to all staff members. I am sure they will not have heard it before. Once you've given this advance warning, you're all set to deal with the next person who displays a lousy attitude. An unsatisfactory evaluation is completely in order for the heater and the negaholic. If improvement is not eminent, further disciplinary action—including dismissal—is justified.

A word of caution is in order. Everybody has a bad-hair day once in a while. The revelation of this chapter is not a license to bust every teacher who gets a little grouchy now and then.

It has been my observation that even when administrators have a clear understanding of this concept, they fail to act. In Maryland, for example, the state law mandates that every principal evaluate teachers on their personality at least once every two years. The law goes on to say that if a principal determines a teacher's personality is unsatisfactory, disciplinary action is mandated. Notwithstanding the very clear mandate of the *Annotated Code of Maryland*, I can't recall one single incident where a teacher was ever rated unsatisfactory and disciplined in accordance with this law. Not one case in twenty-eight years.

Instead, I witnessed several incidents where principals allowed themselves to get sucked into a rather public confrontation with a heater. I recall one principal whose patience wore thin in the front office one morning, and he blurted out, "Goddamn it, Lana Kay, I am sick and tired of your constant bitching!" There were other teachers, support staff, and even parents in the office at the time. Guess who got his butt in a sling over this one?

I am reminded of an old story that goes something like this: "If you are standing on a street corner and you get into an argument with some jerk, will the passerby in the car know which one is which?"

THE FARMER'S WIFE

No, it wasn't Old McDonald, but it was a farmer's wife in a little old elementary school way out in the country. She had a history of exploding at the drop of a hat. Whoever was around at the time got the brunt of her nasty outburst. Virtually every teacher on the faculty had been victim to her behavior at one time or another. Most of the time it happened in the faculty room, but occasionally it occurred in the hallway or the parking lot.

On this particular occasion, it happened in the classroom in front of the kids. Angered and embarrassed, the receiving teacher marched straight down to the office and demanded action. It didn't take long for the principal to document a laundry list of complaints from several staff members. Loaded with ammo, the principal met with the farmer's wife and proceeded to take the appropriate steps, culminating in writing a letter of reprimand.

It didn't take the teacher long to find her way to the union office. "I have been at that school longer than anyone else on the faculty, including that principal," she lectured. I got to see firsthand what the letter of reprimand was all about. After a few minutes of her bluster, I was able to get a word in edgewise. "Are the allegations true?" was the only question I needed to ask. She couldn't deny any of the incidents and really didn't try to justify them at all. She just didn't see what the big deal was all about. After all, everybody lets off steam once and a while.

I explained the job security implications of a poor personality and the state of the law in this regard. She was quite surprised to learn just how serious her situation had become. I knew we could never win a grievance over this letter since the principal and the teachers had thoroughly documented her offensive behavior. She quickly realized that her only option was to change her ways or face dismissal.

This story has a happy ending: The farmer's wife got the message, lasted another two years without another serious outburst, and retired to her farm. The last I heard she was living happily there and was just as content as her Black Angus steers grazing in the pasture. Some said her case was a testament to the principal's resolve. Others merely passed it off to the power of Xanax.

So here's the deal. Don't act like the old ostrich. Think about your buddy and how he dealt with the farmer's wife. I guarantee you will be the hero of the hour with the rest of your staff. Start by giving some thought to the following questions (and be honest!):

- When was the last time you rated a teacher's formal evaluation satisfactory or unsatisfactory based on his or her personality?
- When was the last time you gave serious consideration to even including personality in your thought process about a teacher's formal evaluation?
- Have you ever seriously considered recommending a teacher for a demotion because of a personality conflict?

If you answered no to each of these questions, you're going to be shocked at this one.

A negative answer to these questions puts you in direct violation of Maryland law. That's right, folks—you are required to evaluate a teacher on his or her personality at least once every two years. You are required to make a specific judgment on every teacher in your school and to take specific action if you conclude that there is a personality problem with any of them. It's a "shall," not a "may"! The *Annotated Code of Maryland* states it very clearly in Section 6-103(d).

So now you know, and you no longer need to put up with the heaters. Disharmony within the workplace is not constitutionally protected. You can therefore take action to eliminate it completely. In the past, you may have dealt with this problem by allowing yourself to get sucked into an argument with the heater. Sometimes your patience wears thin and you just let it loose. At all costs, however, you must avoid criticizing a teacher in front of others. Getting into an argument with the kind of person described here can open that door in a heartbeat, and the next thing you know others hear you and now you're on the defensive.

If you have a heater on your staff, rate him or her unsatisfactory on the next formal evaluation, and begin the dismissal process. You simply don't have to tolerate those constant bad-hair days!

CHAPTER 11

"I Just Can't Do It"

Building the Confidence Necessary to Dismiss

My high school basketball coach had an old saying that he used when we would come up with excuses for not doing what he said. "Can't never did anything," he would bark. I have come to realize that his words were as apropos to teacher dismissal as they were to the basketball court. Listen to the "cant's" I've heard over and over from your colleagues when they have lamented a poor teacher on their faculty. Do they sound familiar?

- "I don't want a grievance filed against me."
- "Who needs a lawsuit?"
- "Would you want the superintendent breathing down your neck?"
- "No way do I want to read my name in the newspaper."
- "A charge of discrimination would ruin my career."
- "When would I find time to dismiss a teacher? I'm too busy running the school."

There just doesn't seem to be a priority commitment to the evaluation process when it comes to the dismissal. I believe this is often caused by a lack of confidence on the part of the principal. As Pogo said, "We have met the enemy, and he is us."

Developing that confidence can begin right here and now. Experts have paved the way. Steven N. Sobel, a nationally recognized professional speaker on motivation, self-esteem, and team building, offers some sage advice. "High self-esteem can result in professional success," he says, which is right on target. High self-esteem can be seen in the amount of fulfillment you derive from your work. Sobel outlines these good tips for improving your self-esteem as well as your professional success:

- Stay away from the energy vampires. These are the negative and sour people you encounter everywhere. Spending time with them drains your own reserve and puts you in a negative mood. Sobel coined the term "negaholics," which perfectly describes the people who center on all the things that can go wrong or do go wrong.
- Surround yourself with nurturing people. These folks are the good listeners and the friends who encourage you to take calculated risks. They make you feel that your judgment or decisions are OK even if they don't work out perfectly.
- Take calculated risks. Self-esteem is often enhanced when you try something new or accept a challenge. It gives you a feeling of confidence and fortitude.
- Develop a philosophy that keeps the past in the past. It is important to live in the present and to look enthusiastically toward the future. The things we get excited about tend to get excited about us. If you want an exciting career, you cannot wait for enthusiasm to come knocking at your door.
- Find good mentors. Select these people on the basis of positive qualities and professional skills. Mentors create high levels of self-esteem and can give you the confidence to try new skills and make decisions without hesitation.
- Self-esteem will grow and the world will be a nicer place if you learn to laugh.

Sobel's message is perfect for those following the advice and theory of *Dismissal Doesn't Have to Be Difficult.*

CHAPTER 12

Don't Pass Up the Gimmes

Learn What They Are and What to Do about Them

Once you have identified a teacher who needs to be removed from your school, it is important to scour the field for reasons to justify your decision. Quite frequently, the incompetent teacher leaves a trail of unsatisfactory performances that are often overlooked. The point is when you are handed one of these gimmes, don't let it get away. It has been my observation that this happens all the time, so it might be that principals and supervisors don't recognize these gifts. In this chapter, I describe those that were most prevalent in my experience.

TEACHER ADMISSION OR AGREEMENT

Anytime a teacher admits to an infraction or agrees with an unsatisfactory observation, document it in writing. Include it in the observation report or in the letter of reprimand or the evaluation document. It doesn't get any better than this. This documentation is obviously unchallengeable. Be sure you date it, time it, and enclose it in quotations.

A good example of this gimme is Perry. He was allowing his boys to play football on the playground, even though the school policies prohibited the activity. When the principal questioned him, he stated that he always allowed the boys to play football, and he thought the policy was ridiculous in the first place. The principal was wise to quote him directly in her written evaluation as well as in the letter of reprimand.

Frequently, teachers will acknowledge that their class was unruly during the observation and sometimes add an explanation. Anytime this happens, be sure to include it in the written report. If the explanation is valid, the quote will speak for itself. If the explanation was a lame excuse, the same will be true.

LEAVING THE CLASS UNATTENDED

This practice seems so obviously wrong, yet it is much more common than one might imagine. Perry provides us with another textbook example of a gimme. Every morning he would get his class settled down, then he would make his rounds, visiting his grade-level teammates. Perry had been doing this for years, and the previous principals probably knew it. In fact, it was a cat-and-mouse game with Perry and his colleagues. They even had a signaling system.

Willful neglect of duty, misconduct in office, lack of executive ability, poor teaching efficiency—pick your poison. You have a teacher dead to rights on any of these causes for action.

OBSERVATION REPORTS

That's right, folks—observation reports. It is a generally accepted theory that you are the expert and you are hired to make a judgment. Unions know they can't match your level of expertise and that appealing the substance of an observation report is usually futile. So as long as you stick to the truth about what you observed and the teaching techniques you are looking for, these reports are clear sailing.

In Maryland, for example, the State Board of Education and the courts have given you carte blanche when it comes to the content of your observation reports. You are virtually untouchable as long as you stick to your professional judgment of what's going on in the classroom. The content of observations has been ruled nongrievable and an illegal subject of negotiations and arbitration. Bottom line: The union can't challenge it. In addition, the state board has made it clear that it will not substitute its judgment for that of the principal.

Granted, most of you aren't as lucky as your counterparts in Maryland, but these venues are still carefully protected rights that come with your position. You are hired to perform this function, and you are recognized as the expert in the evaluation process. So don't overlook this gift.

EVALUATION REPORTS

Exactly the same protection as described for observation reports applies for evaluation reports. It is perhaps the most obvious gimme in your arsenal, yet it is the one most frequently overlooked.

THE CURRICULUM

This is one of those no-brainers. If the district has a curricular mandate, every teacher must follow it. Yet I can't recall any examples of teachers receiving an unsatisfactory rating for failing in this regard, especially as it related to state- or federally mandated assessment tests. Keep in mind these are the very standards by which you are being judged. Therefore, it is in your own best interest not to overlook this gimme.

Let me illustrate this point with a real-life example as it relates to Maryland's assessment test. You make it clear to all of your teachers that you expect to see examples of the test's vocabulary words used in daily lesson objectives, which must be written on the board. (For example, "We will identify fragmented sentences.") This expectation has been clearly communicated time and again.

During your teacher observation, you discover that no such vocabulary words appear on the board or in the teacher's verbal explanation. This observation report should be rated unsatisfactory. It is a gimme's gimme. Of course, it doesn't have to be an assessment test requirement. The same thing applies to any curricular expectation that you have clearly communicated to the staff. With every expectation, there must be consequences for failure to execute.

THEY BOOZE, THEY LOSE

Booze and drugs at school are obvious gimmes, you say, and they are never tolerated. Well, you are wrong. I could cite examples in many school districts of cases involving alcohol or drugs during the past decade.

Now here is a good example of a situation that can be handled differently depending on the competence of the teacher. Recognition that alcoholism and addiction are illnesses can and should result in compassionate responses by the principal, depending on the circumstances. If the teacher in question is a good teacher and is making a sincere effort to provide the kids with a quality education, then I would recommend referral to an employee assistance program as the first step. If, on the other hand, the teacher is in the deadwood category, or the mediocre category combined with some of the more severe disruptive traits described in this book, I would recommend dismissal.

In short, if teachers with these problems are deserving of a second chance and you think it will move them toward excellence, give them a break. If not, don't tolerate their behavior.

The Boiler Room Smelled Sweet

Ted had been using the boiler room as his smoking hideout for years. For about as many years, everybody in the school and the community knew he was deadwood personified. He didn't try to improve, and he flouted the system. Since he was the music teacher, his incompetence became very public at the biannual PTA concert.

Ted came to school late at least twice a week. He would fail to show up for work and wouldn't call in sick. He missed appointments with students, and he never provided a schedule to his principal.

The smell of smoke from the boiler room often was not that of the Marlboro Man, if you get my drift. The sweet smell from the boiler room was matched only by the occasional whiff of alcohol that slipped out despite the overpowering smell of peppermint candy on his breath.

Ted remained on the staff for more than a decade. In fact, he stayed long enough to qualify for retirement. You will read more about Ted in another chapter. But he illustrates the presence of these serious conditions and the fact that these gimmes are often ignored.

Obviously, you must no longer allow a Ted to continue on your staff. Dismissing Ted would be a slam dunk and the union knows it could never win an appeal of a case like this. It is doubtful the union would even try.

THE HIGH FIVE

Principals and supervisors in Maryland have been handed so many gimmes that there should be no deadwood left in any classroom in the state. Likewise, the mediocre teachers should soon vanish. The High Five is the latest gift from the state board. The new certification regulations require that a teacher achieve a satisfactory evaluation in three out of any five years. Without a valid teaching certificate, the teacher cannot remain employed. It is a legal way around tenure.

High Five is a slow process and only recommended for the mediocre performers. A teacher who is at the deadwood level should not be given this much time to continue to destroy the kids' educational opportunities.

This approach is especially suited to the good teacher on a downward slide—in other words, for the teacher who used to be good for the kids and is worthy of redemption. Good teachers are hard to find, and if you can resurrect one, it may be worth the wait. You're the judge. Just be careful not to get lulled into the use of the High Five as a crutch or as another form of avoidance behavior.

OUTRAGEOUS USE OF CLASS TIME

If football is a game of inches, teaching is a game of minutes. Every one of them is precious. In a typical class period of forty-five minutes, a lapse of five minutes is critical, and a waste of fifteen minutes is a crisis. Let me illustrate my point. Stop reading, right now. Look at your clock and sit silently for five minutes.

That was a long time, wasn't it? So, you see, even five minutes of wasted time is a gimme and deserves to be noted. Outrageous waste of student time is cause for dismissal.

Betsy and the Talk Shows

Betsy hadn't even begun her report cards yet and the deadline was at the end of the day. Since she wasn't prepared for her senior English class anyway, she decided to let the kids watch *Oprah*, or maybe it was *Regis and Kathy Lee*. In addition, she figured the seniors were responsible enough to help out with her grading chores—not judging, merely recording.

The atmosphere was light and casual—plenty of time to gossip with the kids about other teachers in the building and the various student love affairs that were on the rocks.

Oops, Betsy didn't count on a principal observation that day. The principal could never have imagined what he was about to witness, never in his wildest dreams. Especially not from a twenty-five-year veteran teacher who was active in the local teachers' union.

Of course, this never happens in your school. Or if it does, you've never been unfortunate enough to see it (or fortunate enough, as the case may be). Clearly, a gimme like this should never slide by.

If, as in the case of Betsy, you have either deadwood or mediocrity at hand, your action can and should be severe. Suspension, dismissal, or at the very least, second-class certification should follow.

If, on the other hand, you discover this outrageous behavior on the part of a good teacher, your action might be less serious. At the very least, an unsatisfactory evaluation for the semester, if not the year, is a must. Avoid the temptation of cutting him or her too much slack. Of course, the probability of finding a good teacher in this boat is very slight. But you never know. You should never pass up the gimmes completely.

IF THEY OFFER TO QUIT, SAY OK

Sometimes a teacher, in a fit of pique or in a moment of self-pity, will say something like, "I get the feeling that you want me to resign" or "If that's the way you feel, I will turn in my resignation." Far too often, a principal backs away and tries to cover this truth so as not to hurt the teacher's feelings or increase the anger.

Don't pass up this gimme. Be careful not to make it look like a pressured resignation or retirement, but definitely affirm the thought and invite the action. This might be a good time to say something like, "Well, maybe that is something you would like to consider. Why don't you think it over and get back to me on that?" Plant the seed. You never know how your garden might grow.

CHAPTER 13

Only the Excellent Teachers Get Tenure
Eliminate the Marginal and Mediocre Nontenured Teachers

There is absolutely no reason for any teacher to attain tenure status unless he or she is an excellent teacher. If your school has a mediocre teacher who achieved tenure under your supervision, we both know who is to blame.

The bar must be raised. We can no longer award tenure to unsatisfactory teachers.

Only the best remain. You will never have problems with the probationary teachers you get rid of. You only have problems with the ones you keep. This is your one free pass—your one chance to separate the chaff from the wheat without concern for union appeals or administrative review. Use it wisely and with critical judgment. The kids are depending on you.

A Maryland probationary teacher has no legal entitlement to a continuing contract. As long as you meet the appropriate deadline dates, all you have to do is notify the teacher that his or her contract is not being renewed for the following year.

Here again, the Maryland State Board of Education is your best friend. It has published guidelines for you to follow in the evaluation process, but it has also assured you that the decision is yours and will not be overturned at that level.

The Maryland State Teachers Association has won only one nontenured case in its history, and that was long ago. Since that lone win, the unions virtually never file an appeal on nontenured cases. They recognize the reality that except for a constitutionally protected violation, there is no chance of winning. The state board has bent over backward to uphold the local school system's right to make the judgment call. The courts are not about to substitute their judgment for that of a trained professional administrator who is paid to do the evaluation.

THE BENGAY CASE

The famous Bengay case will demonstrate the state's commitment to the local's right to make the decision on tenure status. This teacher had received no unsatisfactory observations or evaluations. The Guidelines for Evaluating Probationary Teachers had not been met. They require four separate observations by at least two different administrators as well as two formal evaluations each year. This had not occurred.

In fact, the only negative feedback this guy remembered was when his principal criticized him for coming to school with a strong smell of Bengay. Even so, the principal recommended that this contract not be renewed. The superintendent agreed, and so did the local board of education.

The Maryland State Teachers Association, wary of its chances of winning a nontenured case, decided to take a chance, test the new guidelines for nontenured evaluation, and appeal the case to the state board. In a stunning decision that underscored its commitment to the local control over tenure decisions, the State Board of Education upheld the local principal, ruling that the school system had met "substantial compliance" with its guidelines.

The message from this ruling is dramatic and proves the point of this assertion: There is no reason for any principal to grant tenure to a probationary teacher unless that teacher is first-string varsity quality. Knowing this legal background, I have been shocked and amazed at the number of third-year teacher cases I had to deal with over the years. I recall one that nearly blew my mind.

Here was a third-year teacher bringing me a stack of unsatisfactory observations and evaluations along with a threat to place her on a second-class certificate. (This preceded the recent change in the Maryland law that allows a third year of probationary status under certain circumstances.) I couldn't believe it. This must, I thought, be a meteoric decline in performance for this woman to go from satisfactory to unsatisfactory in just six months.

Upon cursory review of her paperwork, I quickly discovered that my analysis was flawed. Her negative write-ups spanned the entire two and a half years of her career. The system had granted tenure to an unsatisfactory teacher and had now decided to take action. A few months ago it could have ended the problem with the stroke of a pen. Now it would have to waste administrative time to document a course of action. Worse than that, it would expose another class of kids to the damage of an unacceptable teacher. It took two more years to settle this case, when the teacher finally decided to resign.

DON'T TAKE THE THIRD

The new law in Maryland that allows a third year of probation may seem like a good idea on the surface. I believe it will lead to the problem of keeping bad teachers around rather than weeding them out. It will foster avoidance behavior and tempt principals to "give them another chance" and thus put off the tough call. Look, if a teacher hasn't made the varsity level in two years, it isn't likely to happen in three. Do not take this bait.

Actually, this law gives the unions a weapon they never had before. They will argue in every case now that "surely fairness should provide the teacher with another chance." This is just one more layer of pressure and stress that you don't need. So avoid it. Do not fall prey to allowing incompetent or mediocre teachers to "take the third."

I would recommend that you reserve this option for those special cases that you believe will benefit your school and the kids. Don't ever agree to it as a union compromise.

Probationary status in all states is meant to be a trial period. No state grants nontenured teachers equal protection to that of their tenured counterparts. Some states may provide a modicum of due process, but that standard is very easy to overcome. Delaware, for example, allows a nontenured teacher to appeal the recommendation to the superintendent, but not beyond. Obviously, no superintendent is going to overturn a principal's recommendation if he or she has been a part of the coordinated evaluation process as recommended in this book.

If a nontenured teacher hasn't reached excellence by the deadline date for the tenure decision, he or she is never going to make it. Two years is more than enough time for any teacher to prove his or her mettle. Three or four years, which is provided in some states, is icing on the cake.

CHAPTER 14

Tenure Is Not a Firewall
for the Unsatisfactory Teacher

The Most Overrated Myth in Public Education

How many times have you heard someone say, "You can't fire an experienced teacher because of tenure"? How many times have you heard a colleague lament, "If only so-and-so weren't tenured, I would get rid of him or her"? Tenure is the most overrated concept in the history of public education in America. Its perception is its power.

Three decades ago, an NEA staff director told me, "If they ever figure out this myth of tenure, the floodgates will open up." Here it is thirty-two years later, and the tide hasn't even risen. If the NEA never achieved anything else in its long history, creating tenure and perpetuating its power have been its crowning victory.

There is no tenure law in Maryland. How about that for a controversial proclamation? Go ahead, get out your code. Look for the tenure statute. The word *tenure* in the context used here only appears once in the entire thousand pages of the Education Article, and that's just a passing reference in the Professional Negotiations Act. Maryland, like many other states, does not have a tenure law. Our fair-dismissal concept is known as a *continuing contract*. The contract is actually a part of the code and only becomes a continuing one after a probationary period of two to three years.

The belief that teachers have tenure for life, like federal judges, is simply not the case in any state in the nation. Yet the public and many administrators act as if teachers do. As was pointed out in an earlier chapter, any competent administrator can dismiss any incompetent teacher, anytime. It just takes careful planning and thoughtful documentation. Believe me, I have experienced this reality firsthand as a union representative many times in a three-decade career. We never won a tenure case when the administration had done a professional job and the teacher had violated one of the causes for action. This was true in both Delaware and Maryland. If you follow the advice given in this handbook, you will never lose a dismissal case. That is an iron-clad guarantee.

Most state laws parallel Maryland's regarding the grounds for suspension and dismissal—immorality, misconduct in office, insubordination, incompetence, and neglect of duty are always listed. Some states, like Maryland, add "willful" to the neglect grounds and modify others with redundant examples, such as "failure to report suspected child abuse" under misconduct. These additions are almost always made so the legislators can appear politically correct. (For a quick and easy understanding of the terms *incompetency* and *negligence*, check out appendixes B and C.)

The myth of tenure is so pervasive it's scary. Radio talk-show hosts are constantly bemoaning the belief that you can't dismiss teachers in the public schools because of the unions and the tenure laws. The myth of tenure has become engrained into the thinking of our society. Take, for instance, the postmaster in my hometown, who recently read one of my workshop promotional flyers. "You won't sell that idea, because it's impossible to fire a teacher, just like it's impossible to fire a postal worker. It's so complicated and takes so much time that it's just not worth trying. Federal government workers are the same way. Good luck!" he barked, with a shrug of his shoulders and a smirk on his face.

Not surprisingly, his reaction is the most common response I have gotten when I tell people the topic of my project.

MARY A.

Mary A., a very competent, dedicated teacher, was quick to reassure me that she didn't have to worry about her job security because she was tenured. She told me she was untouchable. With ten years under her belt in two different states, she drew her conclusion from firsthand experience and constant reinforcement from her colleagues, her administrators, and her college professors.

When I explained the topic of my workshop and publication, I was intrigued by her response. I expected her to be defensive. But Mary was quick to agree with my premise that there are teachers out there who should be removed. She began enumerating the faculty members she had worked with over the years who should have been dismissed. She backed up her assertion with examples of the teachers' ineffective strategies, and she was particularly animated about one specific teacher.

She then shared the following anecdote, which caused her to be particularly irate.

When the achievement test scores came out, she was quite proud of her students' test scores. All but one of her kids had surpassed the state average in every subject area. One kid fell short of the state average in reading. This student was sent to a reading specialist for instruction throughout the year and thus was not under Mary's tutelage for this subject. And guess what? The reading teacher was the very teacher Mary had described earlier. This saga doesn't end here. Mary went on to explain that everyone in her school knows this teacher should be dismissed, but her principal is too weak to take any action.

TINA

Tina came to visit my son and daughter-in-law for dinner one Sunday. She is a bright, young, enthusiastic high school teacher. My son teased, "Dad, why don't you tell Tina about the book you're writing? Maybe she'll buy a copy." Not one to back down from a challenge, I whipped out my promotional flyer, handed it to her, and watched anxiously for her reaction. Her facial expression and her nodding head telegraphed the response. Again to my amazement, she was nodding yes, and her raised eyebrows told me she, like Mary A., also agreed that ineffective teachers existed and needed to go.

Tina immediately focused on the negativity of a few faculty members at her school who throw a wet blanket on every new idea that she brings up in the lunchroom. She frowned as she told how demoralizing their constant criticism is for her and others who want to give their all to the kids. She was able to quickly name one or two experienced teachers who "had no business being in a classroom." Instead of criticizing my theories, she embraced them and focused on the harm these folks were doing to the kids. She lamented the effect they were having on staff morale, and she bemoaned the fact the "administration couldn't do a thing because they were tenured"!

Tina had just finished her master's program in school administration and was completely indoctrinated in the myth of tenure. She explained that her grad school professors frequently advised their students that upon achieving tenure, they were "home free and couldn't be fired." In fact, the chair of the education department of her college led the pack. In his lectures, he declared flatly that a tenured teacher could not be fired. Tina assured me that her classmates were convinced, as was she, that tenure was a silver bullet for teacher security.

Needless to say, we engaged in an enlightening discussion as I outlined the theory of my work and the myth of tenure. *Disbelief* could best describe Tina's reaction. She was hearing a foreign message, one she had never heard in six years of teacher preparation in the state of Delaware.

PREACHING THE UNTRUE GOSPEL

As a promotional strategy, I joined the state administrators' association as a corporate member. I began placing ads in its publications for my upcoming book and my workshops. Shortly thereafter, I received a copy of the association's annual professional journal and began leafing through the pages looking for interesting articles to read. "Shock and disbelief" is probably a little bit hyperbolic in describing my reaction, but only a little bit, as I turned the page. Here was a feature article, authored by a retired school superintendent, discussing how difficult it was to evaluate teachers and how it was virtually impossible to dismiss one with tenure. He asserted that a principal simply can't successfully document a case sufficient enough to withstand a union challenge. He cautioned principals to tread softly around this challenge and to avoid it at all costs. He argued that dismissal action is an exercise in futility and that danger awaits any supervisor who ventures into this field. He predicted that because of union challenges, very few, if any, tenured teachers in the state would be fired in the years ahead. His article amounts to academic surrender.

Is it any wonder the myth of tenure is so ubiquitous? Our colleges are teaching it, our principals are practicing it, our politicians are preaching it from the pulpit, and our retired administrators are writing it in the scriptures and text.

Unfortunately, the congregation's blind faith has led school systems into the valley of the shadow of mediocrity. The public has bought into the myth, and I believe that most people feel it is fruitless to even try to dislodge an experienced teacher, no matter how terrible his or her teaching has become.

It is interesting to note that many school administrators, and indeed managers in the public sector, ascribe the same mystique of tenure to their entire workforce. They tend to treat all employees in the system with the same trepidation that they treat a tenured teacher. This is especially true in situations where there is a unionized workforce. Most government managers feel it is virtually impossible to dismiss an employee. They cite union confrontation and threats of legal action as insurmountable obstacles.

Ironically, the unions lose far more dismissal cases than they win. We always dreaded dismissal cases because, in truth, we could never win when management did its homework. Management enters the arena cloaked with the advantage of authority. The union enters the ring with the albatross of having to defend the incompetent at any cost. Arbitrators, and the courts, presuppose the expertise and authority of management, especially the school administrator. The law recognizes the legitimate superiority of a supervisor and attributes expert status to his or her testimony. The employee being charged and the union do not come to the table with equal status. It's the word of a professional trained in the art and science of supervision, and afforded the advanced level of educational achievement, versus the lame excuses of a disgruntled employee, fighting to save his or her paycheck.

Think about it for a moment. The teacher has only his or her feeble attempt to explain away incompetence, or misconduct, or whatever the charge. The union brings no cloak of authority and certainly no recognition of educational expertise. It is the word of a loser versus the well-documented professional presentation of a recognized leader in the field. Clearly, advantage management.

Interestingly enough, I have found that some school board organizations are right in sync with my theory. For example, the Pennsylvania School Boards Association (PSBA) has done excellent work in this field. In its copyrighted workshop documents, PSBA declares, "Tenure is not a Teflon shield." The trust of this program, entitled "4 Ds: Documentation, Discipline, Demotion, and Dismissal," is an outstanding training program that admonishes school administrators to weed out the incompetent and ineffective teachers. The association believes that every school organization has at least 5 percent of its teachers in need of the 4 Ds. Public sector critics project 10 percent, and the public puts the percentage much, much higher.

The myth of tenure is the greatest misconception in public education today. Tenure is not a firewall of protection for incompetent teachers. Tenure is used as justification for avoidance behavior. It is a convenient scapegoat, and the myth provides lots of cover for those who don't have the confidence or the inclination to act.

CHAPTER 15

Why Principals Are Reluctant to Act

Learn the Number One Reason
and How to Get around This Obstacle

Over the years, I learned that the problem with getting rid of incompetent teachers didn't always rest at the door to the principal's office. The following incident will put this discovery into focus. It is not necessarily an isolated case.

Our lawyers told this teacher he could not win the appeal. Two of the best criminal attorneys in the state advised him to accept the offer. The state's attorney concurred that he didn't have a prayer in a tenure appeal. The superintendent told me point-blank that he would dismiss the teacher if he didn't agree to resign.

I had negotiated an early retirement buy-out that was better than any offered in the Maryland–Delaware–Virginia region. It was my responsibility to carry the water, avoid the legal challenge, and persuade the teacher to accept the lucrative deal. The hammer was direct and to the point: "If you don't accept it, you will be fired." All the lawyers authorized me to advise the teacher, "If they fire you, we can't win."

The assistant superintendent had done his homework. He had a two-inch-thick file of careful documentation. He had student witnesses. He had parent witnesses. He had teacher witnesses. And he had a paper trail that would lead a blind squirrel to an acorn. This teacher had a history of problems that dated back to his probationary days some twenty-seven years earlier. As a matter of fact, I wondered how the guy ever received a continuing contract in the first place.

Confident that I could settle this case and avoid a lose-lose confrontation, I arranged a conference with the teacher to deliver the good news. This old veteran union representative had his ducks in a row. I could smell that sweet scent of success.

I carefully outlined the terms of the agreement. I emphasized the unanimous opinion of the lawyers. In short, I delivered the ultimatum. This tenured teacher looked me square in the eyes and said, "Mr. Elder, the super has feathers!" After I recoiled from my shock, he further explained that he believed the superintendent was too "chicken" to fire him. I cautioned him not to take the gamble. He turned down the deal—and it turned out he was not fired.

Although it frequently appeared that principals and supervisors were not willing to bite the bullet and do the work necessary to effect a dismissal, the more I researched the issue, the more I found that the weak link in the chain was often in the central office.

Research done at the federal government level shows that the number one reason supervisors do not dismiss unsatisfactory employees is the lack of support and backing from higher levels of management. My anecdotal research done over the years in face-to-face discussions with principals and supervisors shows the same result. Time and again I was told that pursuing a dismissal action wasn't worth it because they did not believe the superintendent would support their effort. In looking back over numerous examples of deadwood that I know should have been removed, it is clear that many were not removed because "the super had feathers."

Let me share an unbelievable story with you about a superintendent whose feathers were so thick you could fill a mattress and have enough left over for the pillows. The principal and vice principal had documented twenty-one incidents of insubordination and misconduct in office against this tenured teacher with twenty-five years under his belt. He had spent all twenty-five years in the same building, while the administrators were relative newcomers to the school. He had established himself as the intimidator, according to the previous vice principal, and no one had ever dared to challenge his self-appointed position. He also was committed to his method of teaching and was not about to change to accommodate the new state performance and assessment program. The principal and vice principal were not about to let him slide. Let the games begin!

Bragging that he saw nothing positive about the new program or the new administrative team, he engaged in a calculated strategy to undermine their credibility. He openly encouraged other faculty members to join his campaign of defiance.

On one occasion he lied to a parent about the rules and regulations for placement in the gifted and talented program. Her son, a student in his class, had failed to meet the requirements for admission, and he deliberately shifted the blame to the administration by misrepresenting the school policies when the mother asked him for an explanation. In reality, it was the teacher's evaluation that prevented the kid from getting in. He saw this as a good way to avoid responsibility for an unpopular decision while at the same time creating a controversy for the principal. Obviously, the parents were upset, and it took weeks for the administration to straighten out the situation.

On another occasion, during a conference with the vice principal, this teacher got angry, stood up, stormed out of the meeting, slammed the door, and flatly refused to finish the conference. He then announced that he would not attend any more meetings with the vice principal unless the principal was also in attendance. He also informed the principal, through her secretary, that he would no longer attend observation conferences with the vice principal.

Just to whet your appetite for one more of his shenanigans, he walked up to the principal and vice principal in the cafeteria and proceeded to tell them an off-color joke of a sexual nature, within earshot of the students. This happened in the middle of the Monica Lewinsky–Bill Clinton fiasco, so you can let your imagination guide you to the graphic nature of the joke he told. You should also know that the school district had a zero tolerance sexual harassment policy that specifically prohibited jokes of a sexual nature in the schools.

Finally, to give you one last good picture of this guy's audacity, he flaunted the schools playground policies, which had been developed by the faculty. He allowed his students to play football during recess even though the school rules clearly banned this activity from the playground, since the faculty thought it was too dangerous.

Wouldn't you know? One of his students broke his collarbone playing football during lunch recess one day and thus exposed the school district to a potential lawsuit. When questioned about the incident, the teacher's only response was that he thought the rule was stupid in the first place and that his kids had been playing football for years during recess.

This incident was the straw that broke the camel's back, so the principal wrote a letter of reprimand, detailing these incidents and eighteen additional examples of insubordination and misconduct in office. She had the vice principal sign the letter for emphasis, and she placed a copy into this teacher's personnel file, all carefully drafted so as not to violate the negotiated contract or any school board policies. She also gave him an unsatisfactory evaluation for the school year. She had done an excellent job of documentation. It was a "slam dunk" winner for the management team.

To her shock and dismay, the superintendent ordered her to change the evaluation to satisfactory and offered these words of advice: "It would be in your best interest to remove that letter from the personnel file." He took this action because the union had filed a grievance, and he was concerned that it might cause a confrontation since the teacher had been such a good employee for so long. In fact, he said, the man had an impeccable record, according to his personnel file, and this report would cause a blemish.

Why would this superintendent display such a lack of courage? I can only speculate. Perhaps it was because he was a rookie superintendent who was afraid of causing a confrontation this early in his career, or perhaps it was because he had a reputation in his previous position as a personnel director who was "someone the union can work with" (i.e., union code words for "pushover"), or perhaps he was just so inexperienced that he really believed he might lose the case to the union.

The sad irony is that the union reps were quaking in their boots. They knew they had a loser. For one thing, in Maryland, evaluations were not even subject to the grievance procedure. The courts had previously ruled that evaluations and observations were an illegal subject of bargaining, so the union was prohibited from pursuing the grievance in the first place. In fact, the union had advised the teacher to be prepared to accept the evaluation and the letter and to be thankful that the principal wasn't pushing for dismissal.

I had to admire the tenacity of these two administrators. They continued to push the issue. Realizing that they had no choice but to accept the superintendent's decision, they concocted a strategy to pressure him into doing something to solve their problem. They raised a mild objection to the decision by insisting that the documentation of the incidents remain within the narrative section of the evaluation. They also pressed for the teacher to be transferred out of the school. The superintendent agreed, once he found that the union would not raise objection.

This principal had successfully removed deadwood from her school, despite the presence of "a super with feathers." The kids in her school would benefit from her commitment.

It is my understanding that the receiving principal soon began to experience the same problems, and the saga started all over again. This time the parents got involved and were putting pressure on the school board members, who were putting pressure on the superintendent. It will be interesting to see if the super still has feathers.

BEWARE THE BOUNCING LEMONS

Bouncing lemons seems like a great idea as long as you're the bouncer. This is the oldest avoidance game in the field of education. It is a favorite of the super with feathers. You may have a bounced lemon on your staff right now. To avoid dismissal of a tenured teacher, the superintendent merely transfers him or her to another school in the system —thus bouncing the lemon from one place to another, hoping that the problem disappears.

Of course, the problem never disappears. It is merely dumped on another principal and on another set of kids. Creative bouncers will move the lemon to the far corner of the system in hopes that the parents don't know.

I especially like the superintendents who pontificate about this dastardly deed when a principal demands that some deadwood be removed from his or her school. I love to hear about the lecture the principal receives: "We won't practice bouncing lemons in this district." This, of course, means that you will have to deal with the problem yourself.

So what to do? Now is the time to put *Dismissal Doesn't Have to Be Difficult* into action. When dealing with a super with feathers, the thing to do is document him or her to death. Don't take the easy route and back down. If you continue to document unsatisfactory performance, the superintendent will be forced to deal with the problem. The more egregious the infractions, the better. Following these steps will protect you in the event something serious happens as a result of the teacher's improper actions.

For example, if you are on record recommending that a teacher be dismissed for improper treatment of the kids and the superintendent does nothing, your documentation will cover your behind in the event of a disaster. You will not be held liable for the superintendent's inaction. By the same token, the superintendent eventually will realize that the teacher problem is not going to go away. He or she will be forced to support you in solving the serious employee problem that you have professionally documented. To ignore it will place the superintendent in an untenable position should the problem blow up. It is at this point that the earlier pontificating you heard about bouncing lemons becomes a revealing test of your superintendent's resolve.

Does your super have feathers? You have proved your case. You have documented your dismissal. The deadwood can no longer remain in your school, and the superintendent knows it. He or she has to act. If the lemons begin to bounce, you will have your answer.

It is always amusing to watch the tough pontificators take the bouncing lemon option rather than the dismissal route. That's when you know your super has feathers.

While this result won't benefit the receiving principal or the school population, it will have achieved your goal. You will have gotten rid of the deadwood in your school, and your kids will be better off for the determined stand you took. You did your job. It is not your fault that your superiors didn't do theirs.

Principals and supervisors must resist the temptation to throw in the towel. You are the front line of defense. Without your commitment to the quality of teachers in our classrooms, our public schools don't have a chance. Most of the research into what makes an effective school points to the quality of the principal. A good principal is necessary to make a good school. This is a proud badge of honor.

It takes a lot of courage to face the hurdles of dealing with a superintendent who has feathers. Look at it as a challenge, not a roadblock. *Dismissal Doesn't Have to Be Difficult* gives you the skill and knowledge to do the job. Following the guidance from these pages, you will be able to overcome the most strenuous opposition from the unions. You will also be able to overcome the most resistant avoidance behavior of the central office staff.

You can't have that world-class school without world-class teachers. You will never have a world-class faculty if you have mediocrity and deadwood on your staff. Most of our future superintendents will come from your ranks. You can guarantee that this problem does not perpetuate itself. Take the "no feathers" pledge!

CHAPTER 16

Don't Worry about Those Outside Organizations

How to Handle Groups with Powerful Initials

Just how much do you really have to worry about those dreaded "initial" groups? You know, the ones that strike fear in your heart when your secretary tells you they're on the line. Those that come to mind from my experience include the NAACP, AFT, ACLU, MSTA, NEA, EEOC, JDL, NCCJ, HEW, USDOE, HRC, and OSHA.

For some reason, we have come to believe that these groups have some sort of mystical power, and if they are involved, we must really be in trouble. In reality, they don't have as much power as you do. You shouldn't worry about them any more than you would worry about dealing with your local PTA president.

Let me state very clearly that I am not casting aspersions on any of these organizations. I am or have been a proud member of some of them for many years. They are all outstanding organizations that have contributed mightily to our country and to our public schools. My point here is that they are nothing more than that. So don't get yourself in a tizzy just because they have entered into the picture on behalf of the deadwood you know must be excised.

No matter how splashy their names sound, they cannot prevail in a case in which you have followed the *Dismissal Doesn't Have to Be Difficult* formula. Keep in mind the admonition we outlined earlier in the book about the kids' welfare, and know, too, that their agent is well aware that he or she is but a passenger aboard the *Titanic* with regard to the case at hand. Furthermore, it has been my experience that all these groups defer to the Maryland State Teachers Association in the final analysis anyway. In thirty-two years, I never saw a case in which any of the groups mentioned took the lead in the defense—or, for that matter, even showed up at the table. None is an expert in school law, and they know it.

More important, *you* are the expert in observation and evaluation and in the documentation of this specific situation. No one—not the union, the superintendent, or the good Lord himself—knows the details and intricacies of this case like you. Remember this the next time you get a phone call from any of the organizations we've mentioned or, for that matter, any we forgot.

There's an old union saying that fits perfectly with the flamethrower concept: "When you got the facts on your side, you pound on the facts. When you don't, you pound on the table!" So when they come at you with their guns blazing, rest easy. This means you've already won. Unions use these dreaded initial groups as a strategy, as a tool of intimidation. Bring in the big guns. Maybe they will back down, because we sure can't win on the facts.

Bottom line: Don't worry about the flamethrowers. They're only hot air, and now that you have studied the KISS theory, they're reduced to a warm summer breeze!

CHAPTER 17

Does the Union Have a Secret Arsenal?

Find Out the Truth behind the Union's Most Powerful Weaponry

The union has only one secret weapon. It manifests itself in many different forms, but there is only one weapon. It is powerful. It is effective. And it has been working for more than fifty years. What is it, you ask?

The union's secret weapon dates back to Franklin Delano Roosevelt. "Crazy," you say. "Hell, this guy must be nuts," you think. "What is going on here?" you ask. Well, let me explain. FDR said, "We have nothing to fear but fear itself." And that's it:

Fear is the union's secret weapon!

And Lordy, Lordy does it ever work. The union counts on it and exploits it very effectively in each and every case. Fear on the part of the building-level administrator, fear on the part of the supervisor, and fear on the part of the superintendent become the union's triangulation. It depends on the resultant confusion to force a compromise or an outright victory.

Earlier we explained the myth of tenure. That myth becomes magnified in the dynamics of the dismissal process. The dreaded initial groups bring added pressure on the different levels of management. When "the super has feathers," the secret weapon has the force of a nuclear missile launched from a stealth bomber. The union will play one against the other and very effectively create doubt in the minds of all. The principal will become fearful that the superintendent will not support his or her action.

The supervisor will worry about the left hand–right hand theory that we covered in chapter 8, fearful that he or she will get caught in the crossfire among the principal, the superintendent, and the union. The superintendent will sweat over the possibility that this issue will end up on the front page of the newspaper just when he or she is ready to begin that major PR offensive aimed at funding a budget. At a time when the management team should be working together in solidarity to improve the quality of the schools, the union will be striving mightily to drive a wedge between these blocks of granite.

Administrators often amplify their fear of being sued, despite the fact that they have complete immunity in carrying out their duties regarding dismissal. Many principals and supervisors forget about this protection. Some may not know about it. Maryland law, Section 6-109, should eliminate this fear completely. "Immunity of school employees from civil liability for certain actions" is the subtitle of the Maryland law, and section (b) specifies immunity for participating in disciplinary, administrative, or other proceedings, including an employee dismissal. Most other states have similar laws, and certainly the principle of implied immunity gives ample protection for administrators to do their job. So you can put that fear to rest.

Frequently I found administrators who were unfamiliar with their own rules, procedures, policies, and contract provisions. I would count on this factor and then use this fear and trepidation to help me succeed.

The administrators would often beat themselves because of their fear and uncertainty. This is what I call "more bluff than stuff" on the part of the union rep. You can see why it works so effectively if the administrator hasn't done his or her homework. You can also see how ridiculous it is to allow yourself to ever be in this boat. If you follow *Dismissal Doesn't Have to Be Difficult*, you won't have to worry about this.

We always practiced the kitchen sink theory when fighting a dismissal case. That is, we would throw in everything but the kitchen sink. We had another way of saying it that may be a little too graphic for some of you but that clarifies the theory quite vividly: "If we throw enough shit against the wall, some of it will stick." That's why the union always charges you with violating the entire contract, all school board policies, all state and federal laws, the constitution, the UN charter, the NATO Treaty, the Bible, the Koran, the Treaty of Versailles, and the bylaws of the World Wrestling Federation!

This strategy has a twofold purpose. First, it is designed to elicit fear on your part by making it seem like you have committed a federal crime. Second, it is designed as a cover-your-butt measure for the union reps in case they missed something in their preparation for the case.

Another favorite variation of this theme is the use of inflammatory words to describe your actions as a principal or supervisor. Flamethrowers are only hot air, remember? As my mother used to say, "Don't let them get your goat."

What's the difference between a witch-hunt and a fair and thorough investigation? The answer is simple: It depends on who signs your paycheck. If the union signs your paycheck, you call it a "witch-hunt." If the school board affixes its John Henry, it's a "fair and thorough investigation." Get used to this reality, and your stress level will drop rather significantly. The union will always accuse you of conducting a witch-hunt even if you had the Dalai Lama doing the documentation. Remember, they've got to pound on the table if they don't have the facts on their side.

You can easily see why it is so important to ground your decisions in that fundamental bedrock theory: It's the kids, stupid. By taking this high road, you can never go wrong, and the union's secret weapon—fear—will explode and be exposed as mere powder!

SANDRA'S SCIENCE WENT SOUTH

Sandra was a third-year teacher in the same school district that I mentioned earlier. She, too, had managed to slide by the nontenure gimme. She was a bright young teacher with a lot of creative energy and an outgoing personality. Unfortunately, Sandra relied on the seat of her pants to get through most of the teaching day.

Other third-grade teachers were frustrated by some of her activities. For example, while their kids were hard at work preparing for the state school performance tests, Sandra's kids were square dancing. She justified this waste of a complete afternoon by declaring that her kids had been working too hard and needed some fun time to relax. Kids in the other classes questioned why they couldn't dance for the afternoon, too.

As is so often the case, a weak teacher's performance affects the entire grade level and maybe the entire school. When Sandra allowed her students to stay out on the playground for extended periods of time, kids from every grade level could see it and would ask for the same break.

One day, as she was getting ready for a leisurely afternoon of play, Sandra looked down the hall and saw her supervisor coming with her note pad. Realizing that she was about to get busted, she quickly grabbed the teacher's manual and told her students to get out their science books. She opened the teacher's edition and began the lesson, flying by the seat of her pants as usual. The topic was the revolution of the Earth around the sun. Terror struck Sandra when she read the word *rotation*, feeling sure it should have said "revolution." The teacher's manual surely couldn't be wrong, so she surmised that she had it mixed up in her rather scatterbrained mind.

She taught the entire lesson incorrectly. She even used the kids to demonstrate how the Earth moved around the sun. Following the incorrect lead of her teacher's edition, she carefully explained to the kids that this was called "rotation." Needless to say, the supervisor was flabbergasted and rated the lesson unsatisfactory.

Sandra called the union with indignation. Over the phone she explained that she received an unsatisfactory for doing exactly what the teacher's manual had instructed. No further details were given, and it sounded like a major injustice had been committed. This may be an exciting case, I thought.

Sandra brought a copy of the observation report and the teacher's manual with her for our conference, as instructed. After I read the observation and the teacher's manual, there was dead silence for what seemed like forever. Could this be for real? Was she serious? Did she actually believe the union would file an appeal?

After schmoozing for a few minutes, I got around to explaining that she didn't have a prayer and that she may very well have exposed herself to serious charges concerning her scholarship, her teaching efficiency, her competence, and on and on. Believe it or not, Sandra persisted in trying to shift the blame to the teacher's manual.

Having taught elementary school in my earlier years, I explained that she couldn't have passed my fifth-grade science class without knowing the difference between rotation and revolution. She, of course, knew the difference, but since she was totally unprepared for the lesson, she had choked and tried to wing it—and she got caught.

We decided to try an age-old tried-and-true lesson in life. When all else fails, try telling the truth—all of it—and ask for another chance.

Fortunately for Sandra, but unfortunately for the kids, her supervisor accepted her apology and agreed to make another observation with the understanding that the unsatisfactory report would be destroyed if the next class went well. The follow-up observation was satisfactory, and the gimme was forfeited.

Did Sandra learn her lesson? No way. Within days she was back to her laissez-faire teaching practices, and as far as I know, she is still dancing away her afternoons in the same school.

Put on your thinking cap!

- Using the theory of *Dismissal Doesn't Have to Be Difficult*, what would you have done in this situation?
- List all of the causes for action you could have documented from this lesson.
- Based on this lesson, do you believe Sandra has the potential for being an excellent teacher? Defend your answer.
- Assuming this lesson was typical of Sandra's performance as a teacher, would you rate her as mediocre, or would you describe her as deadwood? Defend your answer.

CHAPTER 18

Exit Counseling

More Than Just a Euphemism for Firing

"Exit counseling" encompasses a multifaceted, humanistic approach to counseling an unsatisfactory teacher out of the profession. Sometimes referred to as "out counseling" or "counseling out," I prefer to call it exit counseling as a term of art.

Believing I had heard this term used in various conferences, I searched long and hard for its source. After exhausting my research skills, including the Internet, it became obvious that there was not one single reference to this term in a job dismissal context. So it looks like I may have coined a new phrase for our educational jargon—"exit counseling."

Exit counseling is an ongoing process, and it encompasses much more than outright dismissal. It takes into account the human relations aspect of telling someone he or she no longer can remain in a profession that may very well be a part of his or her self-image. It is not easy to do, but it is preferable to a highly charged confrontation.

Beginning with the observation and evaluation process, a teacher who has declined to mediocre or deadwood status is identified. Exit counseling starts immediately and, of course, includes the requisite professional assistance components as well as the documentation phase. You must resist the temptation of avoidance behavior at this early stage. Hoping the problem will go away never works. It will continue to fester, and the longer you wait, the worse it gets. The time has come to step up to the plate and level with the teacher about the severity of your concern. If you practice this up-front approach right from the get-go, you will eliminate virtually all of the union's future claims of unfairness.

In addition, you begin to condition the unsatisfactory teacher to the exit counseling process. He or she must realize that the status quo will no longer be acceptable and that failure to improve will result in dismissal. Remember now, we are dealing with deadwood, not your Teacher of the Year.

Early on, you should begin to mention options for the teacher to consider. These include retirement if he or she qualifies, resignation, change of career, or even a leave of absence for further training if you believe that will bring the teacher up to the level of excellence. Be honest with your assessment of the teacher's chances for success in the assistance component of your counseling. If you honestly believe the teacher can't do it, don't mislead him or her by giving false hope.

Chances are you and your management team will be the only persons shooting straight with this teacher. His or her teaching peers won't. The union won't, and of course, the unsatisfactory teacher in question won't see it or accept it at this stage of the process. If you hide this assessment from the teacher for whatever reason, you are setting into motion a self-destructive set of circumstances that will come back and bite you in the rear end, without fail.

Here is a tried-and-true question to pose early on: "Do you think it might be time for you to consider a career change?" You will be amazed at how frequently the response will be affirmative. I can honestly say that we got an affirmative response more times than not when we were dealing with deadwood. The minute you get a positive response to this query, you can be sure that the exit counseling strategy is on its way to success. Continuation of your game plan will result in a positive atmosphere and a win-win conclusion.

Remember, however, that exit counseling is a two-phase process. It is a carrot-and-stick situation. It won't work if you back off of your documentation of the unsatisfactory performance at this stage of the game. It will be so tempting to "make nice" and let the observation reports slide with a satisfactory rating since the exit strategy appears to be heading in the right direction. Do not make this mistake. It will torpedo your ultimate goal—guaranteed.

Always document your case with the expectation that you will end up on the witness stand being cross-examined by some hot-shot lawyer or on the front page of the daily newspaper. This precaution will prevent you from getting blindsided, and it will also provide the stick to make the carrot look appealing. As you continue the documentation phase, the teacher is becoming more and more conditioned to recognize the inevitable. Also, the more thorough your documentation, the greater the probability that you will never have to use it.

DON'T BE THE LONE RANGER

Always coordinate your exit counseling strategy with your management team. Make sure you avoid a case of the left hand not knowing what the right hand is doing. Your team should speak with one voice. Obviously, this presupposes team agreement on the conclusion that the teacher is unsatisfactory and should be dismissed. This is no time to become the Lone Ranger. (Come to think of it, the Lone Ranger didn't act alone, either. Remember his *kimosabe* Tonto?)

Coordination in no way connotes some kind of nefarious conspiracy. Quite the opposite, it proves the fairness of the evaluation process, and it eliminates the possibility of bias on the part of any one member of the management team. It is a sort of check-and-balance system.

If, however, there is genuine professional disagreement among members of the team over the basic evaluative conclusion, it has to be resolved before going any further. In reality, this scenario seldom happens when you're dealing with deadwood, but if it does occur and you don't correct it, the union will drive a Mack truck through this hole in your case.

Exit counseling should not be viewed as backing off. Using this humanistic approach will help ensure that you achieve your goal. The reality is that an overwhelming majority of the cases you carefully and professionally document will never result in an appeal. The union will see the handwriting on the wall and actually become your ally. I have more experience in this activity than anyone reading this book. It's not easy, but it is rewarding, and everyone comes out a winner.

CHAPTER 19

Don't Let Fairness Become an Albatross
Why You Should Avoid Going Overboard in the Name of Fairness

The Fairness Fantasy is such an easy trap to fall into. You will recall that in the previous chapter, even I advised that you err on the side of fairness when you're conducting your exit counseling process. While that concept is true, you have to be careful that your commitment to fairness does not become an albatross. The union will hammer away at your lack of fairness, especially if you miss a step somewhere along the way, so we don't want to treat it casually, either. To put the concept of fairness into perspective, I believe we need to go back to the basic theory of this handbook.

First and foremost, our commitment to fairness must begin with the kids. Remember that the baseline test for beginning the exit counseling process in the first place was the answer to the simple question "Would I want my son or daughter exposed to this teacher." The entire thrust of *Dismissal Doesn't Have to Be Difficult* is geared to dealing with a no answer to this question. If we stand by this commitment, then we place our focus on fairness right where it should be — it's the kids, stupid! I can't emphasize enough that principals and supervisors need continually to remind themselves that this is the acid test. In reality, nothing else matters.

A variation of this theme should be posed at this point: Is it fair to the kids? Is it fair to the kids to keep this teacher in the classroom? Is it fair to the kids to allow this teacher to continue doing whatever it is you found unacceptable? Make sure that your commitment to fairness begins with the kids; then you can justify your actions regarding the teacher, regardless of the accusations from the union or the flamethrowers who were identified earlier.

"What's fair is fair" and "The issue isn't pay—it's fair play" are two slogans we used over and over again, and they worked every time. Whether the issue was a strike in Harford or Cecil County or a contract impasse in Prince George's County or a teacher dismissal or grievance out in western Maryland, the sound bite caught on, and the public responded in a positive way. Fairness sells. It's common sense. It's motherhood and apple pie. Everybody supports fairness. Certainly, no administrator wants to be on the other side of this campaign. As a result, you bend over backward to make sure that you treat the teacher with fairness—but, unfortunately, sometimes at the expense of the kids.

Perhaps the easiest way to fall into the Fairness Fantasy trap is to allow yourself to be lulled into believing the teacher should be given another chance. After all, it seems only fair that the teacher be given the benefit of the doubt. No one can argue with this logic, and in most cases it makes perfect sense. The problem I observed over the years was that the deadwood often was in his or her tenth or fifteenth year of second chances. This fantasy becomes such an exercise in avoidance behavior. Fairness to this longtime employee is the mantra of the union, and it becomes the salve to ease your pain as well. Each time you are tempted to fall into this trap, go back to the basic question about the kids. If it becomes a choice between fairness to the kids or fairness to the teacher, always choose the kids.

The second most common plunge into the Fairness Fantasy trap is in the realm of due process. Now, obviously I am an advocate of due process and would never advise a school administrator to do anything that could be construed as a violation of the teacher's basic due process rights. Due process rights are specified in the negotiated agreement and the school board policies or in state or federal law. These are the rules, and they must be followed to the letter. On the other hand, you should not go overboard and start handing out due process gifts in the name of fairness. Granting extra appeal meetings or hearings is a good example of a common mistake I observed and participated in over the years. The more often you allow the union up to bat, the better its chances of getting a hit. Naturally, we always appealed to your sense of fairness. Give us another chance to explain. What could that possibly hurt? I can still hear the echoes of my plea in the back of my brain. I used it so often because it almost always worked. There were times, however, that even the union got blindsided by an overzealous administrator who had taken the Fairness Fantasy plunge. In this area, I will never forget Bozie.

BLINDSIDED BY BOZIE

Back in the mid-1990s, Bozie came into my office with a typical tale of woe for a second-year teacher who had been rated unsatisfactory. The tale was unique only in that the superintendent had directly recruited her for this job two years before. She left her previous district with about twenty years under her belt because of this direct appeal by the top administrator. Feeling that this would give her extra insulation, Bozie had never bothered to come to our office to review her two years of unsatisfactory observations until she received the written notice of her nonrenewal.

At that time, the prevailing law on nontenured teacher appeals was crystal clear. No hearings were required unless there was evidence of a violation of the teacher's constitutional rights. There was no right of appeal and no chance of winning for a nontenured teacher. Accordingly, I advised her of her right to resign before the board voted not to renew her contract. She was not satisfied with this advice, demanding that we file an appeal on her behalf. Again, I explained the law and the policy of the school board, which was iron-clad: no hearings, no appeals.

Realizing that this could be one of those causes célèbres, I contacted the director of personnel (the proper title at that time) to reconfirm my advice and the board's policy in these cases. Reassured, I again advised Bozie that she had no chance of appealing the case and told her that requesting a hearing would be counterproductive and in fact detrimental to her cause.

Bozie informed me in no uncertain terms that she was going to see her friend, the superintendent, and that she could not accept my advice. She was sure the superintendent would act out of fairness and allow her to appeal to the board in a formal hearing.

One week later, I received an angry call from the director of personnel demanding to know why I had drafted Bozie's letter of appeal in light of our previous discussions about school board policy. Even though it was signed by Bozie, the letter was written with familiar legalese and technical wording that convinced him that I had a hand in the ghost-written epistle. I had no idea what he was talking about—I had never seen a copy of the letter and had had no contact with Bozie since she stormed out of my office. We both commiserated about who had written the appeal and about how it would be a complete waste of time.

I contacted Bozie, who informed me that one of the flamethrowers (i.e., one of the dreaded initial groups) had helped her draft the letter and would be representing her in the appeal should one be granted. To make matters worse, the superintendent responded positively to Bozie's letter and granted her a public hearing before the board, complete with a date and a location. When I contacted the director of personnel, he was as shocked as I. The superintendent justified the decision on the basis of fairness, feeling that it was only fair to go the extra mile under the circumstances. Since we weren't involved, my only concern was with the precedent being set. The director, by the way, agreed with my assessment.

Two days before the hearing, Bozie called to say that the initial group had backed out of her case, and she needed the union to get her a lawyer for the hearing. She also informed me that she had demanded and had been granted a public hearing before the board. Here we were, stuck. Now all of a sudden it was our hearing—a public debacle—which we had no part in setting up. We had opposed the appeal. We had advised against the hearing. But that Fairness Fantasy trap that the superintendent had fallen into was now coming back to bite all of us in the butt.

It was every bit the disaster we had predicted—front-page news stories, television coverage on the evening news, and a nontenured teacher who not only lost her job but because of the publicity lost her chance of getting another job in a hundred-square-mile radius. Unfortunately, too, several professional administrators were needlessly put through the wringer of testimony and cross-examination in the glare of television and news reporters, merely because the superintendent fell into the Fairness Fantasy trap.

SAM'S SECOND CHANCES

Sam was a very nice guy. He loved the kids, and the kids loved him. He had tremendous rapport with the parents in the school's neighborhood. He was a team player and was always willing to help out with school functions, even on the weekends. On the faculty for fifteen years, he was popular with the other staff members at his school.

The problem was that Sam could not speak one sentence without making at least three or four grammatical errors. How he ever graduated from college is a mystery. He couldn't possibly have passed English I or English II. His written work was worse. In addition to grammatical errors, he couldn't spell. Report card comments were riddled with errors. Notes he sent home were embarrassing, to say the least.

Somewhere along the line, a new principal caught onto this problem and began a series of classroom observations during his language arts lessons. Sam taught fifth grade in a self-contained classroom. The observations revealed the worst of the new principal's suspicions. The supervisors were alerted, and before long, it became obvious that Sam would have to be given unsatisfactory observations and evaluations. Sam was clearly informed about the reasons for his unsatisfactory performance. How could he teach fifth-grade language arts when he couldn't even model proper grammar?

On the other hand, Sam was a good guy. The kids loved him. The parents loved him, and he had tenure, having been around for more than a decade. He surely deserved another chance. He was given a second chance and a third, and a fourth, and a fifth.

It wasn't until his fifteenth year of teaching and the arrival of another new principal that Sam was finally recommended for dismissal.

Our lawyers hammered away at the fact that he had been allowed to remain on first-class status for fifteen years. The school system looked foolish to have given Sam so many second chances. It was quite embarrassing as it all made the local papers. Needless to say, the local board upheld the dismissal, and the state board followed suit. The state board did, however, admonish the local system for having allowed so many kids to have suffered for so many years at the hands of such an incompetent role model.

I recall that at the state board hearing, Sam's plight was pitifully exposed by the hearing examiner. He read back a few excerpts of Sam's testimony from the transcript, complete with the many grammatical errors Sam had made on the witness stand. The examiner asked Sam to tell him what was wrong with the testimony he had just read. Sam looked puzzled and in fact could not identify any grammatical errors he had made just minutes before. It was so sad. In fact, the union lawyer actually argued that Sam should be granted another chance, but this time with tutoring from a high school English teacher to improve his use of proper grammar. Obviously, the state board did not buy that one.

Sam's case is a perfect illustration of the Fairness Fantasy run amok. It is an extreme example, but, unfortunately, it is real.

CHAPTER 20

Being a Buddy or Being a Boss

What Research Says about the Good Guys

Perhaps the most difficult adjustment any administrator has to make is the transition from buddy to boss. One day you're a teacher sharing jokes in the faculty room with your colleagues, taking part in the gossip about the superintendent and telling the story about using sick leave for a fishing trip. The next day you're their principal sharing your evaluation of their teaching performance. Wow, what a change. "It remains a difficult paradigm shift. . . . [T]he friend who becomes a boss remains one of the most challenging relationships we face in the workplace," according to Tara Parker-Pope and Kyle Pope, in their *Wall Street Journal* article entitled "Who's the Boss Now? Your Friend." They believe the most difficult aspect of this relationship is "the constant shifting of gears from friendship to professionalism . . . a relationship that exists on two levels and it has to shift back and forth very quickly."

Even if the transition isn't that immediate, the line is blurred and tough to maintain. There are mixed feelings on both sides of that line.

Lawrence L. Steinmetz, in his book *Nice Guys Finish Last: Management Myths and Reality*, argues that you can't be the employees' buddy and be a good manager, too. There is a line that can't be crossed, much like the line between teacher and student. "Good guys make bum bosses" is more than a theory. It is a discovery the author has made in his study of employee–employer relationships.

While Steinmetz's findings were not done in a public school setting, I believe his research is valid in the field of education. Think back to the cases I have cited in this handbook. Most of the poor administrative decisions the cases illustrate were made by "good guys." These principals and supervisors just couldn't make the tough call. They didn't want to push the envelope and cause hard feelings. It was more important to keep the peace than to do what was right.

Let's see how you fit in this picture. Take a look at these questions and do some self-evaluation:

- Have you written a letter of reprimand in the past two years?
- Have you rated a tenured teacher's evaluation unsatisfactory in the last three years?
- Have you denied tenure to any teacher in the past few years?

A little introspection is good for all of us. If you answered no to all three questions, there is a good chance Steinmetz might be talking about you. Remember, you're not in a popularity contest with your faculty. Maintaining good staff morale is not based on whether the staff members like you. It is based on whether they respect you. There is a big difference.

CHAPTER 21

The Politics of Teacher Dismissal

Recognizing the Political Realities of Dismissal
and Learning How to Deal with Them

No book about teacher dismissal would be complete without addressing the political aspects of this issue. Politics sometimes dictate staffing decisions and not too infrequently account for the presence of mediocre teachers in the classroom. We're not talking about partisan politics but rather the pressures that come into play when faced with a difficult dismissal decision.

Sometimes school superintendents need more hands than an octopus has tentacles, to juggle the competing political interests, and the myriad of consequences, connected with firing an employee. They get pressure from the school board, the community, the fiscal authorities, the politicians, and the unions. If they please one group, they alienate another. When a tenured teacher gets dismissed, these factors often become magnified tenfold. What seems like a clear-cut dismissal case to the building principal, may become a cause célèbre because of the politics involved. And sometimes these political pressures make the superintendent look like he or she has feathers, when, in fact, a decision not to dismiss may be in the best interest of the school system at this particular time.

Remember "Ted"? His principal hand-delivered a file of documentation two inches thick backing up his recommendation of dismissal. It was time to cut Ted loose.

The documentation was solid and the cause was just. In fact, Ted's dismissal was long overdue, and the principal was confident it would be a done deal. He was disappointed when the superintendent called to tell him the case would have to be put on hold, but he understood the political pressures that had caused the central office to back off that particular year.

Ted was an African American teacher, and the superintendent was in the middle of another dismissal case involving a minority teacher. Even though the principal had ironclad documentation proving Ted's incompetence, it just wasn't politically possible to fire him during that school year.

(To complete this story, you should know that a few years later another principal brought dismissal recommendations against Ted. This same superintendent supported the move. The documentation was so solid and so overwhelming that Ted and his union did not even file an appeal. Instead, Ted took a disability retirement and left the system.)

I've had dozens of principals tell me over the years that they avoided unsatisfactory ratings for minority teachers, whom they knew to be incompetent, out of fear for the political repercussions such a rating might cause. Likewise, I've had dozens of principals tell me they avoided unsatisfactory ratings for other incompetent teachers, who fit into certain categories.

For example, religious and ethnic considerations are equally volatile, and administrators often shy away from dismissal recommendations in those circumstances where a teacher may raise religion or ethnicity as an issue. Whether it is a born-again Christian, a Shiite Muslim, an Orthodox Jew, a devout Catholic, a Zen Buddhist, or some unknown religion from Timbuktu, there is a tendency to bestow supertenure on these teachers. I've seen it many times. Fear of being politically incorrect, or fear of being accused of discrimination, has a greater priority that dismissing an incompetent teacher. Now would be a good time for you to reflect on the case of "Kathy, Kathy, Kathy" in chapter 1. You may want to reread it with the new realization that she was a minority teacher. It may shed some light on the absence of any negative evaluation documents in her file.

The untouchables are another category of teachers whom administrators treat with kid gloves. The untouchables might conjure up images of Elliott Ness or the caste system in India, but that's not who we're talking about here. No, sir. We're talking about a fact of life in our public schools. Certain incompetent teachers are the untouchables, and woe be it unto the principal who dares to cross this Rubicon. "Not on my watch," you say. Well, let's see who might be included in this august group. The superintendent's wife, the school board president's daughter, the senator's girlfriend, the mayor's brother, the civil rights leader's dad, the other principal's son, and your minister's fiancée are among the classic examples that come to mind. These are the kinds of political realities that are often viewed as impossible obstacles. Believe me, the union will pounce on this area and will stretch the concept to include the fourth cousin of the brother-in-law of the mayor's stepmother when devising its defense strategy.

Far too often, administrators treat union officials and union activists with the same deference. I know of many, many teachers who became active in the union for this very reason. In fact, I even had one union president ask me to intervene on her behalf, to stave off an observation, because she was unprepared for the next day's classes. Administrators tend to act as if the union has some kind of magic wand to fight for its leaders, and thus they avoid this voodoo at all costs. It might surprise you, but I know that many of the union leaders I worked with over the years were marginal teachers, and some were downright incompetent. Sometimes, leadership positions in the teachers association became a magnet for the mediocre.

Principals are subject to many of the same political considerations as the superintendent. But they have additional layers to worry about. They have considerable interplay with the local school community, the PTA, the local civic clubs, as well as the local elected officials and political leaders. Then, too, principals have to deal with the popularity of the teachers whom they may find in need of discipline or dismissal, particularly if the teacher is also a successful coach.

Central office politics need to be considered by the principal when thinking about a dismissal recommendation. Is the superintendent in the middle of some bigger controversy? Is the school board embroiled in some districtwide dispute? Is the assistant superintendent willing to go to bat for your recommendations at this time? Is someone jockeying for someone else's job at the board office?

Dismissing a tenured teacher has a unique set of political pressures, and no administrator can afford to treat these realities lightly. Recognizing their existence, however, should not be synonymous with viewing them as insurmountable. Deadwood and mediocrity in the classroom will eventually cause the whole system to collapse. This is why school administrators must strive mightily to avoid the temptation of hiding behind the wall of politics when it comes to dismissing an incompetent teacher.

In the retail field, there is an old saying: "Sales cover a multitude of sins." In the dismissal field, I'd like to offer a new saying: "Documentation exposes a multitude of sins." Therein lies the answer. How do you deal with the politics of dismissal? How do you handle the untouchables? Document! Document! Document! Careful documentation of incompetence, or misconduct, or neglect, or insubordination, or immorality, will eventually overshadow the protection of politics. It will even bring down the untouchables. Just tell it like it is, and then tell it like it is again. Sooner or later the truth will come out. And, in the final analysis, you will be just fine if you follow the advice of the Beach Boys—that is, "Be true to your school."

CHAPTER 22

How to Avoid Grievances

The RAW Method

How do we avoid grievances? Ahh, that's the question! If I've been asked this question once, I've been asked it a thousand times. Most administrators view grievances as an act of war. That's how I devised the acronym for my quick and easy answer to this question. *War* spelled backward is *raw*. *RAW* stands for read, anticipate, win—that's my method, which will be explained in detail. For now, however, a little background is in order.

I worked with two superintendents over the years whom I viewed as the best in the field, yet they were complete opposites in form and style. Not surprisingly, their philosophies on grievance processing were poles apart as well.

Bill Middleton, the superintendent of a rural school district on the eastern shore of Maryland was the master of grievance avoidance. He could resolve a conflict and make everybody feel as though they had won. Win-win was his middle name, and he would go out of his way to avoid having a grievance filed. Now, don't get me wrong—he didn't cave in. He just had a unique ability to see both sides of a coin. In fact, I truly believe that Bill could see the edges, the sides, and the corners of an issue as well.

He promoted this same philosophy among his principals and supervisors. He expected problems to be resolved at the lowest possible level. Working for the union in this environment was especially rewarding. Instead of confrontation, we viewed problems as a collaborative challenge. We were able to maintain a positive labor–management atmosphere. On those rare occasions when a formal grievance couldn't be avoided, we were able to work through it without the usual theater of high-charged animosity.

During his thirty-plus years as either superintendent or personnel director, Bill had only one grievance ever appealed to arbitration.

At the other end of the Chesapeake Bay, Dr. A. A. Roberty held forth with another philosophy of grievance processing. Roberty was the other "best superintendent" I had the pleasure of dealing with, but his philosophy was as far away from Bill Middleton's as was his distance up the bay.

I've heard from reliable sources that Roberty told his principals and vice principals that they weren't doing their jobs if they didn't have grievances filed against them. He believed that strong management and firm contract enforcement may very well have provoked grievances, but that was just fine. Like the old saw about the navy captain who believed that a happy sailor was a complaining sailor, Roberty apparently viewed grievance processing as a healthy sign that the system was alive and well. Once the contract was negotiated, he would stake out his interpretation of the language, and that would be the line in the sand. If the union disagreed, the grievance procedure was the way to iron it out. One principal told me that Roberty would back his managers all the way to the Supreme Court, and that knowledge gave them the courage to stand firm in the face of a union challenge. Several cases, in fact, ended up before arbitrators, the state board of education, or the courts. I must admit that management won most of the appeals, and as a result, the union became very wary of filing grievances, especially those that might have otherwise been filed just to make a point.

Both of these superintendents were masters of their grievance-processing approach. Both resolved most of their problems to the satisfaction of their side of the table. And both approaches addressed the central question posed in this chapter. So, take your pick, and show that you care enough to model the very best.

I will also tell you that I worked with local association leaders who viewed grievance processing from those same opposite poles. Some union leaders would rather fight than win, and they were the ones who viewed success by the number of grievance filed against the school district. I recall one union staffer who celebrated the nation's bicentennial by advocating that his members file two hundred grievances that year. And I remember the president of one of the largest education associations in the nation who was more interested in filing formal grievances than he was in solving teachers' problems.

The leaders of another very large local viewed the issue from the opposite perspective. They practiced a win-win philosophy, consciously working to avoid grievances at all cost. To these leaders, it made more sense to focus on problem solving at the lowest and most informal level.

The point is, avoiding grievances may have more to do with the philosophy of the association leaders in your district than it does with the actions of your management team.

THE RAW METHOD

My simple three-step strategy to help you avoid grievances is the RAW method. The three steps are read, anticipate, and win. By practicing this plan of action, you will take control of this agenda; and, as you will recall, "He who controls the agenda, controls the outcome."

Read!

The number one step, and without question the most important step, is to read, read, and read. Read the negotiated agreement. Read the board policies and procedures. Read the state law. Read the court rulings and state board decisions. You must become the resident expert on all of the rules and regulations, particularly the union contract.

Most teachers don't read their contract. Believe me, I know this to be true. Union building reps aren't much better. Unfortunately, many administrators don't read them, either, until a grievance is filed. At this point it is too late. As I pointed out earlier in the book, I used to count on this factor when I represented teachers.

Take a look at your negotiated agreement, right now. Are the pages crisp and clean and unwrinkled? If so, guess who needs to initiate step 1?

Anticipate!

Anticipate the reaction of your teachers prior to making any decision that may affect their terms and conditions of employment. Anticipate the reaction of the association as well. Then make your decision accordingly. Now, don't get me wrong. I am not suggesting that you back away from making any decision merely because you anticipate a negative response. What I am suggesting is a smart way to do it, so as to put you in control of the situation. It is kind of like scenario planning. You should automatically incorporate this step into your decision-making process.

I recall one principal who illustrated this concept perfectly. He decided to require the teachers to remain on duty all day, for field day, thus eliminating any planning time that the contract required. Concern for the students' safety required maximum supervision by the teachers. Allowing planning time would reduce the amount of supervision and increase the risk that some kid would get hurt. There was an obvious liability concern involved.

This principal anticipated a negative reaction from a few of his teachers. They would claim a contract violation of their planning time rights. So, he contacted the association in advance. He explained the problem and convinced the union rep that, under the circumstances, an exception to the usual daily routine was warranted. He worked out an arrangement whereby the teachers would be afforded extra time off, at a future date, in exchange for giving up planning time on this particular day.

Since he knew the contract by heart, he also was able to point out that the planning time provision specified a weekly minimum rather than a daily guarantee. In reality, he didn't even have to offer the compensatory time deal to effectuate his field day plan, but by offering a sweetener, he could solve the problem in a positive way.

Win!

The best way to avoid grievances is to win the ones that do get filed. By following the advice offered in this book about documentation, and the steps of the RAW method, you will load up your arsenal so fully that you are virtually guaranteed a victory every time a grievance is filed.

Unions hate to lose. When a union rep sees management winning most of its cases, he or she thinks twice before plunging into the fray. You see, selling union membership is based largely on touting its successes. Teachers pay a lot of money each year for dues, usually about $500. The unions can't sell membership on a losing track record. In addition, teachers resent seeing their hard-earned dollars going down a rat hole on some losing cause.

Proof of my assertion can be found in association training these days. Instead of blind advocacy and open confrontation of the seventies and eighties, UniServ directors are now being schooled in win-win negotiations and collaborative decision making.

So, begin practicing the RAW Method today. Focus on winning those grievances that do get filed, and before long, you will find that those dreaded grievances are but a memory of days gone by.

CHAPTER 23

Peer Assistance and Review Program

Is It Right for You?

Let me make one thing clear: I enthusiastically endorse any program that has as its goal the removal of deadwood and mediocrity from the classrooms of our public schools. Peer Assistance and Review (hereafter referred to as PAR) in Montgomery County, Maryland, for example, is a very positive initiative by the superintendent of schools, Dr. Jerry Weast, who recognized the need to address this issue. His research closely parallels the quotes in this book that any organization has about 5 percent of its employees who are not measuring up. Actually, Weast cites 4 percent, but it is a very significant recognition on his part. Rather than react like an ostrich, he faced the problem head-on and decided to do something about it.

I should point out that Montgomery County is one of the wealthiest counties in the nation. Teacher pay is among the best in the United States. This school district has been recognized as one of the best in the country for a long time. So if this school system has about 4 percent of its teachers doing less than satisfactory work, I believe it is fair to suggest that every district should take a look in their closet.

I have discovered, however, that this realization is not always the case. While presenting at various workshops throughout the country, I have encountered more than a few administrators who take exception to my assertion that we all have some housecleaning to do. I recall an incident a few years back when I was addressing a statewide conference on the theory of this book. One human resources director shouted out, "We don't have any deadwood in our district." He wasn't kidding. He was offended by my 5 percent assertion, which was based on solid research by the state school boards association in Pennsylvania.

Now back to PAR. If you are seriously considering one for your district, look to Maryland and not Ohio for your model. You don't have to reinvent the wheel. Montgomery County's plan is the best I've seen, and the following analysis will show you why I recommend it over the Columbus, Ohio, program.

Weast has carefully crafted a PAR that protects his management rights while at the same time provides large doses of union input. The collaborative efforts of the local teachers' association, the local administrators' association, and the superintendent of schools resulted in a package covering all of the bases. Figure 23.1, a flowchart prepared by the Montgomery County Public Schools, will give you a quick yet thorough overview of a successful PAR model.

To get more details on the plan, call (301) 279-3853, or e-mail the public information division of the Montgomery County school system at Brian_Porter@mcpsmd.org, and the very competent director will be most cooperative in supplying you with printed material on the PAR.

Now let's back up, and in the words of that famous philosopher, Maria from *The Sound of Music*, "Let's start at the very beginning, a very good place to start."

One of the cornerstones of the NEA's "new unionism" concept is its Peer Assistance and Review Program. In a nutshell, the program calls for a joint NEA–school board committee to provide support for teachers who need assistance and to make recommendations that may negatively affect the continued employment of those teachers. In other words, you will allow the union to share in the process of evaluating teachers and in counseling out those who you jointly decide should go. On the surface, it sounds like a noble effort on the NEA's part. It certainly appears to be a departure from the traditional trade union mentality, which mandates blind advocacy to any union member without regard to the competence of the teacher involved.

The program calls for extensive assistance for teachers in trouble and lots of time for that assistance to work. We all agree that assistance must be offered in most cases. In fact, NEA's *Guidelines* place the priority emphasis on assistance rather than review.

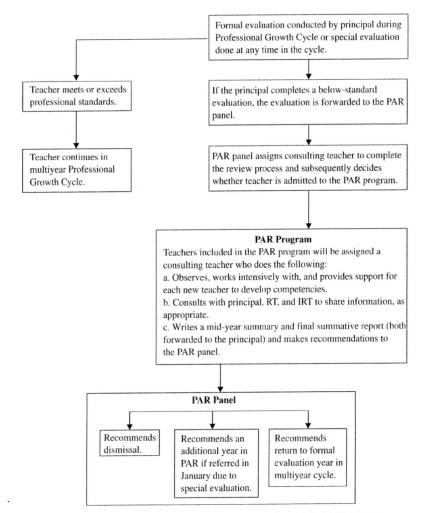

Figure 23.1.   Peer Assistance and Review Program. Copyright 2003. Montgomery County Public Schools. Used with permission.

Let's examine the union's position as a teacher advocate. Dues are high, and members expect protection for those big bucks. I believe it is fair to say that NEA's commitment to PAR is a commitment to avoidance of dismissal for its members who have fallen below the standard of satisfactory. If the union had its druthers, no one would get fired. Former NEA president Bob Chase, who initiated the new unionism philosophy, said it best: "The union will . . . provide help from union designated mentor teachers . . . and in the rare cases where the coaching doesn't work we can recommend dismissal." Please note: Chase says "rare cases."

This program may be particularly attractive to administrators who prefer to work cooperatively at all times rather than face the stress of confrontation. Collaborating with the union in the improvement of instruction sounds great from a public relations standpoint. This may be a grand slam opportunity to achieve your goal of weeding out the deadwood and upgrading the mediocre teachers, while at the same time taking the high road.

On the other hand, is it realistic to expect the union to agree with your assessment? What if the person happens to be a union officer? Let's examine the makeup of the committee according to NEA's plan. The union president will appoint its committee members. Will they be teachers who have been evaluated as excellent teachers or teachers who have been active in supporting the union? You are a certified administrator with professional training and skill in the art of supervision and evaluation. Will committee members now on equal standing with you bring that same level of competence to the table?

MARY B. MAKES MY MESSAGE

Mary B. was the president of one of the hundred largest local associations in the nation. She was recognized as the leader of a very effective local union. She was featured more than once in state and national union publications as a spokesperson for one union cause or another. She was a full-time union president with a leave of absence from her teaching job. Popular and friendly, Mary appeared to be the ideal local leader who could make the PAR program work. She was not a confrontational unionist and she would make the appointments to the joint committee. Since it would be a model project, it is likely she would serve on the joint committee herself. So far all of this sounds ideal, right?

Here's the catch. Last year, Mary was in the classroom teaching while running for the office of union president. She had been rated unsatisfactory for the past two years by her principal and at least two other supervisors. They were recommending that her teaching certificate be rated second class. She was a mediocre teacher at best and more than likely deadwood, despite her long tenure in the system. Her performance in the classroom was a detriment to the kids. Winning the union election saved her career.

Something is wrong with this picture. Would you want Mary to serve as an equal on your review committee to help you judge the competence of your teachers? Would you trust her judgment in appointing the members of your joint committee? Would you be sharing your professional judgment with a professional equal? Is Mary the exception, or is Mary the rule? Do you want to take that chance?

Dismissal Doesn't Have to Be Difficult comes down on the side of caution. Will entering into this joint arrangement foster the KISS theory, or will it place yet another roadblock in the way of excellence in your school? Will it help the kids, or will it expose them to mediocrity for a longer period of time? Before entering into a PAR project with the union, study the personalities of your local union leaders.

It has been my observation that the union was frequently a magnet for the mediocre and sometimes worse. More than a few of the union leaders I worked with over the years were clearly not good teachers. Many admitted that they ran for office just to escape the classroom. And if you take a look at the large percentage of released-time presidents who never returned to their teaching jobs after their terms were over, you can see what I mean. In at least one case, teachers in a president's home school actually petitioned the superintendent not to reassign her back to their school, because they felt she was not a competent member of their faculty. The principal and the superintendent concurred, and she never returned to the school nor to teaching.

You may have seen another variation on this theme in your own district. The union wins a grievance for a marginal teacher, and the next thing you know he or she is a union activist. These wins make for good membership promotion fodder, and the union will frequently put the show on the road. Before long, this mediocre grievant becomes an officer in the local or state association.

The point is quite simple. Local union leaders are the folks you must take on board as equal partners if you agree to PAR. That's the way the process works.

NEA's true position on PAR is ambivalent at best. While the leaders proclaim its virtues, the policy is much less direct. It doesn't specifically endorse the concept but, rather, pledges to support its local affiliates that wish to begin PAR. NEA policy also clearly pledges to make sure that "no member is denied legal representation/assistance through the association's legal service program as a result of participation in such programs." Translation: The union will still fight you in court if you fire a teacher, and it will further the union cause—even if you have a PAR!

These guidelines focus on shifting power away from management and to the union in the evaluation process. For example, the PAR consulting teachers or mentors, the keystone to any PAR's success, shall be appointed by the union, as will the union members of the PAR panel. You will find that its bargaining proposal will demand majority representation on the panel just like its flagship local PAR in Columbus, Ohio.

Furthermore, the *Guidelines* demand extensive training and extra pay for the consulting teachers (CTs) and other trainers as well as full release from their regular assignments. Naturally, they will demand that all rules and regulations be included in the collective bargaining agreement and subject to grievance arbitration.

So let's see. If you agree to the NEA boilerplate language, your local union will take over your evaluation process and who you can fire.

Administrators need to be aware of these goals when you enter into negotiations over a local PAR. Later in this chapter, I will compare and contrast the Montgomery County plan with the Columbus, Ohio, project so you can see why it is best to look to Maryland for your model. For now, let's continue to examine the NEA's new unionism in a historic context—a little trip down education's memory lane, you might say.

Everything old is new again. If you keep those old clothes long enough, they'll come back in style. And so it is with NEA philosophy. The new unionism we're hearing so much about is in reality a warmed-up version of traditional NEA programs that were abandoned back in the 1960s. When the American Federation of Teachers, AFL-CIO, successfully challenged NEA throughout the country, the association abandoned its so-called administrator-dominated programs and set out to "outunion the union." Survival was its motive then. Survival is its motive now. In the 1960s, the threat was losing its members to a competing union. Today, the threat is to public education itself. The stakes have never been higher.

Peer review isn't new. It's been around at the university level for a hundred years. In fact, NEA embraced the concept when attempting to organize higher education in the late sixties and early seventies. But that was just an aside. The real peer review that NEA championed came in the form of its Commission on Professional Rights and Responsibilities (PR&R), with its own semiautonomous executive director. In those days, NEA power emanated from the threat of sanctions from the PR&R Commission.

As part of this program, every state association formed its own PR&R committee with the primary function of handling the teacher dismissal and suspension issues in the state. No association legal or financial support was provided to any teacher without PR&R approval. Large NEA affiliates formed their own committees and followed the state and national policies. A committee was appointed by the association president, and that committee made a judgment call on whether to represent a member who was being suspended or fired by a local school system. The committee included superintendents, principals, and teachers. It was definitely a joint management–union effort. Committee members or its staff conducted interviews with the local superintendent, the principal, and the teacher being disciplined. On-site visits and classroom observations were sometimes done as a part of the investigation. After a thorough inquiry, the PR&R committee would decide by majority vote whether the teacher's case had merit or whether the superintendent was justified in his or her dismissal recommendation.

At times, the committee would recommend coaching for a teacher rather than dismissal. Usually, the local system would follow that advice, as it respected the PR&R's credibility.

Union members were not guaranteed a free ride in those days. Reasoned advocacy and peer review would best describe the union's policy.

The AFT challenge changed all of that. Citing this process as proof of NEA's administrator dominance, the PR&R concept was wiped off the face of the NEA earth. When it set out to prove the AFT wrong, it wiped out all vestiges of reasoned advocacy and professional collaboration with school administrators. We were advocates, not judges. Confrontation with the school board and the superintendent was the way to win the hearts and minds of the rank and file. And that philosophy served the association well for the next forty years. Having lived through these dramatic changes as an association staff member, I can tell you it was quite a ride.

So you see, new unionism and PAR are kind of like NEA going back to its roots. But don't be misled—it isn't shedding its cloak of old unionism anytime soon. To its credit, NEA and its large affiliates like the Montgomery County Education Association are out in front of the membership on this paradigm shift. But don't lose sight of the fact that the *Guidelines* clearly guarantee the members the right to use union legal services to challenge any dismissal action.

Back to the future. NEA's affiliate in Montgomery County made big headlines in the *Washington Post* a few years ago when it negotiated a PAR with the board of education. The superintendent and the union president boasted about the new culture and the new commitment to weeding out the poor teachers. Even the NEA president got in on the press action and pledged the national group's support for the project.

MONTGOMERY COUNTY PAR: AN ANALYSIS

A careful analysis of the leading PAR programs in the country leads me to conclude that Montgomery County's should be the lighthouse for school administrators to look to for guidance.

Since its been in operation now for more than three years, we can clearly evaluate how it is going. You can't argue with success: 110 teachers were dismissed, nonrenewed, or chose to resign following introduction of the PAR process. This is more than twice the number of such teachers in the previous five years, according to information released by Superintendent Weast. Not too shabby, huh?

A close look at the numbers show that a large majority of these folks saw the handwriting on the wall and called it quits when they were faced with the PAR challenge. Fewer than a dozen chose to stick around and face dismissal. These statistics are not surprising. They parallel my experiences over the years. They also support the beauty of exit counseling as explained in an earlier chapter. If you follow the advice in this book, in most cases you won't have to do battle.

Montgomery's PAR, like the one in Columbus, relies on the CTs as the key to its success. These highly skilled, highly trained teachers provide direct instructional support to teachers who have been identified as needing help. Through formal observation, they gather information that is used to evaluate the teacher's progress. Intensive on-site assistance is provided. Since the CT is a colleague rather than supervisor, the suggestions and constructive criticisms are better received. It's like Mary Poppins said: "Just a spoonful of sugar helps the medicine go down!"

I think this is a good point to emphasize as one of the major reasons I recommend Montgomery over Columbus. The CTs are the key to both programs. But in the Ohio model, they are appointed by the union. In Maryland, they are chosen by the superintendent. This is a dramatic difference in philosophy. In fact, in an NEA video highlighting the Columbus plan, the union president makes a point of identifying the CTs as union appointees.

The Montgomery PAR program is overseen by a PAR panel consisting of sixteen members; eight are recommended by the teachers union, and eight are suggested by the administrator's association. The superintendent appoints the members of the panel. Here is another very important distinction between Maryland and Ohio. In Columbus, the union appoints its panel members. In Montgomery County, the union recommends the nominees. Believe me, there is a big difference between recommending and appointing. This is another major management right that you must protect.

Also, in Columbus the union president is automatically a member of the panel, and from the video, it is apparent that he is the chairperson. He clearly comes across in the film as the man in charge.

Another essential difference in the two plans lies in the makeup of the PAR panel itself. In the Columbus plan, the panel consists of seven members; four are appointed by the union, and three are appointed by the superintendent. It doesn't take a rocket scientist to figure this one out.

An essential management protection does appear in both plans, which is good. Make sure you take careful note of this factor. Both PARs have a dynamite clause. A *dynamite clause* is like a contract escape mechanism. If the superintendent—or the union, for that matter—concludes that the PAR is not living up to expectations, it can be exploded (i.e., terminated) merely by giving notice to the other party, with a specified number of days stipulated.

Perhaps the Montgomery County PAR is superior because it was initiated from a management perspective. According to the district's information officer, it was conceived and developed under the major reforms introduced by Superintendent Weast as part of a comprehensive effort to improve the professional development and evaluation of teachers. He remains an enthusiastic supporter of maintaining a rigorous teacher evaluation process and a continuous program of professional development, of which the PAR program is a key component. At the other end of the spectrum, the Columbus plan was initiated by the union.

Before you accuse me of becoming a cheerleader for PAR and for Montgomery County's plan, let me flip the coin for a while. Entering into a PAR program requires a new culture of thinking. You must accept the notion that supervision can best be done by fellow teachers. Of course, if you believe in cooperative teaching for students, you surely believe in the same concept for teachers. I recognize this is a giant leap. After all, you are turning over the most critical area of supervision and observation to the CTs. You're going to have to do a lot of soul searching over the question of what to do with your supervisory staff and supervisory philosophy. If you replace your supervisors with CTs, you reduce your management team significantly. These folks are union members, not managers. Of course, there are serious budgetary concerns over keeping both.

I suggest you shell out a few bucks and purchase the NEA video. View it with your management team and your board of education president before you go any further in your PAR project. It will be a very enlightening twenty-six minutes.

TEN MILLION REASONS TO FORGET ABOUT PAR

Hey, buddy, can you spare a dime? How about $10 million? That's right, folks. PAR is an expensive baby. Montgomery County spends over $10 million per year on the program, according to *Education World*'s feature article on the plan. If you reduce that to a per-teacher cost, it comes out to about $90,000 per year. You know that old saw: A million here, a million there, and pretty soon you're talking about some serious money.

But everyone agrees: To make PAR work, you can't cut corners. You have to pay for the backbone of the program, the CTs, and they have to be trained by staff development experts. You will need lots of money to pay for substitutes to provide the released time to make the program go. As I have clearly indicated, the Montgomery County PAR is the best. To get the best, you gotta spend the big bucks.

I realize that very few school districts share the luxury of being in one of the wealthiest communities in the world. Columbus certainly isn't, however, so it is doable if you have the desire to make it a priority.

The bottom line is this: Caution is still my best advice. Each district must assess its relationship with its local union. It's not the big boys and girls at the national level who you will be dealing with. PAR cannot succeed without collaboration. Collaboration cannot be achieved with a confrontation-oriented union.

Remember, too, that Montgomery County is one of the largest school districts in the nation with more than 9,700 teachers. The local NEA affiliate is one of the most sophisticated in the country with a professional staff larger than most school districts' central office. And while the number of unsatisfactory teachers being removed in Montgomery is impressive, when you apply the percentages to most school districts in the United States, it works out to about one or one and a half teachers per year. You may not find it necessary to establish a PAR in your school district to achieve this same level of deadwood removal.

CHAPTER 24

My Most Memorable Cases

Learn from These True Stories

Over the course of a three-decade career I ran across some very interesting cases. Administrators have told me they enjoy the stories I share during my workshops. In this chapter, I relate my most memorable and some say my most unbelievable anecdotes.

A GOOD-BYE KISS

A kiss in class, and it is good-bye, teacher's job. That's what happened to one tenured teacher several years ago when he allowed a nonstudent to visit his girlfriend during lunch period. The girl was a ninth-grade student in this teacher's homeroom, and the boyfriend was a seventeen-year-old former student who had dropped out of school. This teacher knew the girl's dad did not approve of the relationship, but he had befriended the former student and made his classroom available for these unapproved liaisons. He also ignored the school policy that prohibited former students from visiting students on school property during the school day.

The two lovers didn't hesitate to show their affection for one another. They hugged and kissed in front of the other students, and their behavior became somewhat of a sideshow for the lunch crowd. Some of the kids went home and told their parents, who became upset, and one irate mother called the principal to protest.

Needless to say, the principal was horrified at the teacher's behavior. He consulted with the superintendent of schools, and the teacher was fired. The teacher argued that he wasn't aware of the school policy and that his actions were designed to prevent the girl from dropping out of school.

The union appealed his case to the highest level in the state, arguing that the punishment was too harsh. The argument fell on deaf ears. His dismissal was based on neglect of duty, misconduct in office, and incompetency.

PSYCHOLOGIST, HEAL THYSELF!

A school psychologist who can't interpret tests doesn't belong in the public schools, according to a school district in my distant past. Believing the systems-only psychologist to be ineffective, one superintendent created quite a stir when he attempted to remove the man from the system. Borrowing a procedure that seemed to come straight from the Keystone Cops, this school chief almost snatched defeat from the jaws of victory, and that's what brought the association's Professional Rights and Responsibilities Commission into the picture.

Back in those days, we didn't automatically defend a member just because he or she got into trouble. We practiced a system known as "reasoned advocacy," and we made a judgment call before deciding whether to take the case. In this particular case, we never even got to the merits of the competency issue because the superintendent's actions were so biased and unfair that the whole case was tainted. He had called the psychologist into his office and pressured him to resign or else. He gave him ten minutes to decide, and he wouldn't allow him to contact the association for advice. By the time the psychologist came to us, he had already resigned from his job, under duress. The commission investigated the matter and found that his story was true. So when the district rescinded the resignation and subsequently brought dismissal charges, the association felt obligated to defend its member on due process issues alone.

This time the superintendent did his homework well. He hired one of the state's leading psychologists to review the test results, and the subsequent recommendations, of the school psychologist. Test after test was scored incorrectly. Most of the referrals and recommendations made by the district counselor were faulty as well. It became clear that the school psychologist was unable to properly administer the various psychological tests. Despite the gallant efforts of the association's legal team, the dismissal was sustained by the board of education and the courts. He was fired for incompetency, misconduct in office, and negligence.

A HAIRY MATTER

The board was beaten by the beard. That's what the headlines in the local papers said after the association intervened on behalf of a coach who had been fired for growing a beard. This was back in the 1960s, and the era of constitutional protections for teachers had just begun. A small school district superintendent didn't like the idea of some hirsute hippy leading a basketball team. His teaching job was not involved.

The association was anxious to fight this case for two reasons. First, the stakes weren't that high. It was only his extracurricular assignment, not his teaching career at stake, so losing this case wouldn't be earth-shattering. Second, the organization wanted to begin winning some constitutional cases to plow some new ground in the field of teacher protections.

Armed with lots of court cases provided by NEA's legal department, I appeared before a public meeting of the school board. The First Amendment precedents had already been set by federal courts throughout the land. By the end of the meeting, the board could see the handwriting on the wall. It reversed the superintendent's ruling, and the bearded coach went on to coach his team to a winning season.

TO DIRECT OR NOT TO DIRECT

The play's the thing. Refusing to direct the play, however, was more than the principal could bear. He recommended dismissal and the superintendent agreed. This teacher was given another chance to comply. She refused and was fired for insubordination. The association had no choice but to appeal the case since its rep had advised the teacher to take this stand.

Negotiations were only in its infancy in Maryland at the time, and the issue of voluntary assignment to extracurricular activities was one of the hot topics of the day. The unions wanted to use this case to establish the legal basis for its claim. By winning this case, it could set a precedent for the entire state and avoid dozens of confrontations with other school boards. On the other side of the table, the school board was bound and determined to fight this case to the bitter end for exactly the opposite end result. All eyes were on the county and this case.

The teacher was dismissed, and, of course, her pay and benefits were stopped. What the union thought would be a quick and easy victory, however, became a year-long test of wills. The teacher's expectations were soon shattered, and she began to blame the association for her dilemma.

Meanwhile, other local districts grew impatient and began ironing out their own solutions at the bargaining table. Before long, the statewide importance of the issue faded, and both sides began to reconsider their hard-line positions.

The state organization recognized its culpability in giving such ill–thought-out advice to the teacher in the first place. So it turned to its outside legal counsel to work out a deal. A compromise was reached whereby the teacher was reinstated, but the board retained its prerogative to require teachers to perform extra duties beyond the normal school day.

The association leaders breathed a big sigh of relief and never again advised a teacher to refuse a direct order from management.

A TEACHER BEHIND BARS

Getting paid while serving time in prison isn't what you'd normally think of as sound fiscal policy for a school system. But that's what happened when one superintendent cited the wrong sections of state law when he dismissed a tenured teacher.

A teacher in this district was found guilty of manslaughter and sentenced to prison for running over a sailor with his car. I will spare you the details of this sordid affair, but needless to say, he couldn't report for work. The superintendent notified the teacher, by certified mail, that he was being dismissed. He cited incompetency as the reason, in accordance with the state law. Unfortunately, this teacher had an impeccable record as an extremely effective teacher. His classroom performance was exemplary.

After consultation with my superiors in Baltimore, it became my dubious honor to inform this superintendent that we would be appealing his recommendation, because he cited the wrong sections of the law. I arranged the meeting and awaited the fireworks. Like a Fourth of July extravaganza, the explosion erupted. "How can the association justify defending this guy?" he demanded. "What in the name of God has happened to the profession?"

The bottom line was this: In his haste to clear the system of this teacher, the superintendent had overlooked the obvious. He could have cited neglect of duty, misconduct in office, immorality, or even insubordination, and it would have been a done deal. Realizing the public embarrassment an appeal would cause, his only choice was to work out a compromise. In exchange for a letter of resignation, the teacher would remain on the payroll for the rest of the year.

I personally carried the paperwork to the prisoner, met with him behind bars, and secured his signature for the deal. This was the first of my three experiences of meeting with teachers in prison.

DAVID BEATS GOLIATH

Parental threats don't always hold up as justification for a teacher's unusual behavior. I learned this lesson the hard way in a hearing before the state board of education. A six foot six, two hundred pound tenured teacher was suspended for misconduct in office for mistreating his students as well as their parents. For example, he intimidated the little fourth graders by walking around the room with a yardstick and smashing it down on their desks if they misbehaved. He also placed one kid in a closet for punishment. On conference night, he required the parents to sit ten feet away from him in a student's desk and chair while he held forth behind the teacher's desk. He explained that he did this to protect himself, as one of the parents had threatened to punch him in the face. The teacher, by the way, was a former marine and a black belt in karate.

I was sitting at the conference table with this teacher and our lawyer waiting for the state board hearing to begin. Through the door came the school board's lawyer, the superintendent, the principal, and a bevy of witnesses. The teacher nudged me in the ribs with his elbow. "Here he comes!" he said excitedly. "Here comes that kid's dad, the one who threatened me," he exclaimed. To my absolute horror, I looked up, and there, walking through the door with a cane, was a frail sixty-year-old man, who looked as though he had suffered a stroke. I looked at our attorney, and all she could say was, "Shit!"

Needless to say, we lost that case. There is, however, an important lesson to be learned from this case, and the superintendent in this district learned it well. Why go through all of the hassle of two levels of appeals for a mere suspension? There was no doubt that the state board would have reached the same conclusion even if the penalty would have been dismissal. About three years later, the school system had to do it all over again with this same teacher. This time, however, they fired him, and he lost all of his appeals.

A LESSON IN ROMANCE

A bottle of Chianti and a little poetry make for a lovely evening of romance. But not when it's sent to a sixteen-year-old girl by a forty-year-old male teacher. Love letters, wine, and a little cheese were the evidence one irate mother brought into the superintendent's office. A tenured teacher had sent them to her daughter through the mail. He suggested that the young girl use the code name "Captain Cory" when she referred to him in her correspondence. Several exchanges had taken place, and a meeting was in the offing.

The superintendent called me instantaneously. "Get Captain Cory, and get his ass in here this afternoon!" he demanded. I didn't know what in the world he was talking about, so he filled me in briefly. Since this teacher had a history of this kind of allegation, I wasn't totally surprised. The code name, however, was a new wrinkle in his modus operandi, and the system had never had written documentation in the past. On the way to the board of education office, the teacher confessed to the incident. However, he didn't think it was out of line since the girl wasn't in his class.

Naturally, the superintendent brought dismissal charges, citing misconduct in office and negligence.

Realizing we didn't stand a prayer of winning this one, I engaged in an intensive dose of exit counseling. Captain Cory finally saw the light and resigned from his teaching position.

GOING BY THE BOOK

"The book" is how the teachers referred to the library in one high school where the librarian was being dismissed. Their joke wasn't far off target. I went to investigate and when I got there, the cupboard was bare, so to speak. The library shelves looked like a used book store the day after its annual 75 percent off sale. In addition, the books were so poorly organized that finding a book was like a game of hide and seek.

Among other things, the librarian was being fired for her failure to maintain the Dewey decimal system properly and for her failure to "weed" out the discarded book titles from the card file. Students were complaining. Teachers were complaining, and the principal was tired of "working with her."

I felt sorry for this elderly widow because she had been the librarian at this school for the past twenty-seven years. She needed three more years to qualify for retirement. But the media center was a disaster, and it was all her fault. The administration cited negligence, incompetence, and misconduct in office as the basis for its dismissal charges, and she was removed immediately from the school.

SEX AT SCHOOL

Sex, lies, and videotapes—all topics of cases I handled dealing with the issue of sex between teachers and students. Ranging from prison terms to civil suits, teachers have paid a heavy price for this transgression.

Perhaps the most bizarre was the forty-year-old woman who had sex with two middle school brothers at the same time, while her mother-in-law slept in an adjacent bedroom. She admitted all of this to me, and when I told her I didn't have client counsel immunity, she abruptly resigned. Of course, dismissal charges had already been filed. Obviously, this situation occurred in the late 1960s because if it had happened after the child abuse statutes were enacted, she would have gone to jail.

As I reflect on the many dismissal cases covered in this book, I find an interesting phenomenon. All were outrageous. Most came about only after parental complaints had been lodged against the teacher. And while I averaged about one case per year, very few were based on plain old unsatisfactory teaching. The point is, school administrators did not generally initiate action to dismiss a teacher. They only reacted to pressure from outside sources—and, as the career summary in this chapter indicates, only in the most extreme situations where failure to act would have been unthinkable.

CHAPTER 25

Frequently Asked Questions

Q. *What is the best evaluation format?*
A. Checklist instruments are best. Use only two ratings, S and U (for satisfactory and unsatisfactory). List the items you want to measure, followed by the rating. Allow space for comments, commendations, and recommendations on the same line with each item. Remember, I believe we must raise the bar on our definition of *satisfactory*. Its synonym should be *superior* or *excellent*.

Q. *But shouldn't you have a column for "excellent"?*
A. No. It telegraphs to the teacher that less than excellence is acceptable. For outstanding performance above and beyond, you can make note of it in the narrative section of the evaluation form. This approach will also meet your needs if you have a merit pay plan in your district.

Q. *What do you think are the worst kind of evaluation instruments?*
A. Narrative types. They are a godsend for the union representative.

Q. *How do we know what disciplinary action to recommend for the unsatisfactory performance?*
A. Arbitrators advise that managers always seek the maximum discipline appropriate for the offense. This allows room for the superintendent, the board, and/or the arbitrator to decide on a lighter penalty. You will have to go through the same hassle for a letter of reprimand

appeal as you will for a dismissal, so you might as well make it worth your while.

Q. *How should we handle complaints about teachers made by other teachers or other staff members in the school?*
A. Get the complaints in writing with their signature. Do not act until you get the written complaint. Do not act on nameless, faceless complaints. I could fill three pages with stories about principals who followed through on teacher-against-teacher complaints, only to have the complaining person back down when the heat got turned on.

Q. *What is the first thing I should do if I feel the need to begin exit counseling in my school?*
A. Read. Read the contract. Study all board and administrative policies, rules, and procedures for evaluation. Get your ducks in a row before you start. Be sure to learn the deadline dates.

Q. *If a teacher does something that warrants disciplinary action, should I have a conference with him or her before writing it up?*
A. Yes, if at all possible. Give him or her a chance to explain his or her side of the story. Plan for this conference as you would for teaching a lesson. Know your objective, and make sure you cover all points. Take careful notes, and read back what the teacher had to say, making sure you captured his or her words accurately. Sum up before you stand up. Follow the conference with a written communication specifically covering the incident and the disciplinary action you are taking. Require his or her signature with date and time to acknowledge receipt of the write-up.

Q. *Can you recommend any other publications that discuss dismissal?*
A. Yes. The best I have seen is a workshop document done by Don Owens, of the Pennsylvania School Boards Association, entitled "4 D's: Documentation, Discipline, Demotion, and Dismissal." He also authored an excellent article on the subject in the May 1977 issue of *PSBA Educational Management Guidelines.*

Q. *Aren't you being disloyal to the union by writing this handbook?*
A. No, quite the opposite. The better trained the administration is in fair dismissal practices, the better equipped both sides will be to improve the quality of education in America. In fact, *Dismissal Doesn't Have to Be Difficult* is on the cutting edge of the NEA's new unionism via the Peer Assistance and Review Program, and what its Montgomery County (Md.) affiliate refers to as the "new culture" in labor–management relations. Assuming the NEA is serious about the new unionism's quest to help eliminate unsatisfactory teachers (which I truly believe it is), I would expect the NEA to welcome this book with open arms and to endorse it as the perfect training manual for the joint peer assistance and review consultants.

Q. *If we are convinced we have deadwood in our school, should we go straight for a dismissal action?*
A. Don't jump the gun. Managers should practice progressive discipline, except in the most severe cases. Start with unsatisfactory observations. Then move to unsatisfactory evaluations. Then progress to second-class certification or suspension. And then move to the ultimate discipline—dismissal.

Q. *Should we allow union representation in meetings to discuss disciplinary action?*
A. Yes. I recommend you advise the teacher to bring union representation because the meeting may involve or will involve possible discipline action. This way you eliminate any union challenge of denial of due process. (Check with the board's director of labor relations to make sure that my advice isn't in conflict with district policy).

Q. *Do you have any advice on how to handle the meeting if the union representative shows up?*
A. Yes. Just like you would if he or she didn't show up. It's *your* meeting. It's not a hearing. Plan the agenda. Whoever controls the agenda controls the outcome.

Q. *Should my assistant principal or supervisor attend the meeting. too?*
A. Yes.

Q. *I've been told that it takes too much time to dismiss a tenured teacher. Is that true?*
A. No. It really doesn't take that much additional time. You merely change the focus of your efforts. You have to do the evaluations anyway. It doesn't take any more time to rate it unsatisfactory than it does to mark it satisfactory. And if the teacher isn't measuring up, you have to suggest methods of improvement and provide help in either case. The only way it would take more time is if you are currently ignoring these teachers and allowing them to slide completely.

Q. *Should we allow union representation at evaluation conferences or at conferences when we discuss an improvement plan with a teacher?*
A. No. Not unless the union contract requires it. No need for confrontation at meetings dealing with curricular matters. Union reps virtually never bring expertise to this arena.

Q. *How do we deal with a student complaint of verbal abuse by a teacher when it never happens during our classroom visits?*
A. I experienced many cases in which the administration successfully utilized student testimony to prove its charges. Careful investigation is required to validate the student's complaint, which you must get in writing. Make sure you give the teacher ample opportunity to rebut these allegations before you take action. In all of the cases I dealt with, the administration brought more than one student to the witness table, thus bolstering the credibility of the complaints.

Q. *I agree that we should dismiss the deadwood in our classroom, but what should we do about the marginal teachers?*
A. You should subject them to the exit counseling process just like the deadwood. Sometimes, an excellent teacher will slide toward mediocrity. This action plan may provide enough of a shock to get the teacher back on track. Other marginal teachers will never make the grade. In either case, a marginal teacher should not be permitted to remain in the classroom.

Q. *Your theory is too simplistic. We don't pay enough to attract the excellent teachers. How can we worry about dismissal when we can barely fill our vacancies?*

A. That's what I call the "warm body in a cold classroom syndrome." If that is your recruiting mind-set, that's exactly what you'll get. Even the poorest school districts cannot allow incompetent teachers in their classrooms. I'd rather subject my kids to a different teacher every year than to expose them to an incompetent one year after year. At least this way they have a chance of getting some excellence.

Q. *What is the most valuable advice anyone ever gave you about employer–employee relations?*

A. An old man on the construction crew I worked with in the summer of 1960 gave me this pearl of wisdom: "Right is right and wrong ain't nobody."

The Dismissal Doesn't Have to Be Difficult *Checklist*

Follow these simple steps:

- Banish fear and doubt from your mind. Recognize dismissal as a positive and professional process necessary to improve the quality of instruction for the kids.
- Read. Then read some more. Read the contract, the administrative procedures, and the board policies. Know the deadline dates and the time limits.
- Rate observation and evaluation documents "unsatisfactory."
- Clearly and concisely communicate expectations, deficiencies, and consequences with straightforward, direct language, making crystal clear that dismissal will be recommended if significant improvement is not demonstrated.
- Keep your cool at all times.
- Conduct a fair and thorough investigation.
- Document, document, document. Carefully document your findings in writing, using discretion and brevity as your guide. Don't write or say anything that you wouldn't want to read on the front page of your local newspaper.
- Present your findings in a conference, and give the teacher an opportunity to respond.
- Give the teacher specific, concise directives about what he or she must do to improve. Offer adequate assistance, and allow ample time for improvement to take place.

- Always involve your assistant or fellow administrator in any meeting with the teacher and/or his or her union representative.
- Coordinate your efforts with your management team to eliminate inconsistencies.
- Practice humanistic exit counseling at all times.
- Use progressive discipline where appropriate, but always recommend the maximum disciplinary action at each step along the way, so that the dismissal recommendation will be the natural culmination of the process.
- Safeguard due process, but don't go overboard with the Fairness Fantasy.
- Sleep well knowing that your decision will result in a better education for the kids in your school.

Incompetency Defined

Incompetency is often thought of as an illusive concept. Quite the opposite is true. It has become a term of art, with very specific types of conduct that support charges of incompetency. Donald B. Owen, the associate executive director of the Pennsylvania School Boards Association, has done an excellent job of defining incompetency in an article published in the *PSBA Educational Management Guidelines* in May 1977. In words that cannot be improved upon, he writes:

> Incompetency is generally defined as an incapacity to teach arising out of either a lack of substantive knowledge of the subjects to be taught, a lack of ability or a lack of desire to teach according to proper methodology. It also encompasses deficiencies in personality, composure, judgment and attitude.

Based primarily on Owen's article, I have come up with the following list of actions that have been upheld consistently by the courts as dismissible offenses under the charge of incompetency:

- Failure to maintain proper relationships with students
- Lack of classroom control and discipline
- Poor quality or accuracy of required reports
- Failure to give proper or sufficient tests
- Inadequate lesson plans and/or implementation of same
- Deficient student records
- Lack of ability to motivate students

- Failure to maintain good working relationship with school staff
- Carelessness with confidential student records and/or other confidential records or information
- Lack of proper pacing
- Excessive unexplained absenteeism
- Inappropriate responses to situations
- Poor grammar
- Failure to execute a completed lesson in the time period allotted
- Failure to exhibit the basic components of a satisfactory lesson, such as proper motivation, stating objectives, and appropriate closure
- Failure to recognize obvious symptoms of suspected child abuse or outright examples of sexual harassment by students

Negligence Defined

Negligence, persistent negligence, neglect of duty, or *willful neglect of duty* are terms of art that appear, in one form or another, in virtually all teacher tenure laws. While the concept may seem to define itself, a rather impressive list of examples has developed over the years as a result of court cases throughout the nation. Here again, Donald Owen's article in the May 1977 *PSBA Management Guidelines* provides a good source for most of these examples.

The following actions have been consistently upheld by courts of competent jurisdiction as dismissible offenses under the negligence charge:

- Lateness
- Leaving a class unattended
- Ignoring disciplinary policies
- Swearing at the boss
- Verbal outbursts at a supervisor
- Lack of proper lesson planning
- Improper storage of dangerous materials
- Lack of classroom control
- Refusal to answer questions from management
- Improper release of students from class
- Failure to comply with testing, record keeping, or curricular requirements
- Refusal and/or failure to follow an order

- Failure to submit reports and/or not doing reports in a timely manner
- Leaving school early without prior approval or notification
- Excessive absenteeism without good cause
- Sleeping in class or during meetings
- Improper disciplining of a student
- Refusal or failure to accept an assignment
- Misuse of class time
- False statements in an attempt to use sick leave or personal leave
- Transporting students at excessive speeds and/or in violation of district policy
- Impropriety of teacher–student relationship
- Failure to attend meetings or inservice workshops
- Allowing unauthorized persons in the classroom or school activity
- Swearing at parents, students, or other staff members
- Failure to supply required verification for illness or other absences
- Showing up for work in an inappropriate state of dress or grooming
- Failure to report suspected child abuse to proper authorities
- Failure to report sexual harassment to proper authorities
- Failure to intervene appropriately in student fights

Cases Summarized

Bibliography

Adams, Brooks Henry. "A Teacher Affects Eternity." In *Annotated Code of Maryland*. Education, 1992 Replacement Volume, 1995 Supplement. Annapolis, Md.: Department of Education, 1992, 1995. (Also available at www.memorablequotations.com, *The Education of Henry Adams*, chap. 20, College of Liberal Arts & Science, University of Illinois, Urbana.)

Berra, Yogi. *You Can Observe a Lot by Watching*. Little Falls, N.J.: LTD Enterprises, March 1998.

Cromwell, Sharon. "Making Teacher Evaluations Work." *Education World*, May 6, 1993.

Daugherty, Carroll R. "The Seven Tests of Just Cause." In *Take Sides! How to Win Teacher Grievances*, ed. Roger P. Kuhn. Los Angeles: California Teachers Association, Southern Section, 1970.

Dyer, Wayne W. *Your Sacred Self*. New York: Harper, 1995.

Goleman, Daniel P. *Emotional Intelligence*. New York: Bantam, 1995.

If Teachers Fail: Fix or Fire. Video. Washington, D.C.: NEA Professional Library, School Stories, Discovery Communications, 1997.

National Association of Elementary School Principals. *Streamlined Seminars* 17, no. 4 (June 1999).

National Education Association. *NEA Handbook, 1997–98*.Washington, D.C.: Author, 1997.

———. "Peer Assistance and Review Program." In *NEA Guide for Local Affiliates*. Washington, D.C.: Author, December 1999.

Owen, Donald. *PSBA Management Guidelines* 6, no. 3 (May 1977).

Pennsylvania School Boards Association. "4 Ds: Documentation, Discipline, Demotion, and Dismissal." Workshop manual. Harrisburg: Author, 2001.

Pope, Kyle, and Parker-Pope Tara. "Who's the Boss Now? Your Friend." *Wall Street Journal*, February 17, 2002.

Sobel, Steven N. *High Impact Seminars*. Springfield, Mass.: New England In-
    stitute for Stress Management, 1995.

Steinmetz, Lawrence L. *Nice Guys Finish Last: Management Myths and Re-
    ality*. Old Greenwich, Conn.: Devin-Adair, 1983.

William of Occam. *Occam's Razor*. WorldNet 2.0 DICT Development Group,
    Elements Database 20001107, January 29, 2001; available at www.
    ucsub.colorado.edu.komineki/elements.

Index

About the Author

Chet H. Elder retired from the Maryland State Teachers Association in 1998, having served thirty-two years as a UniServ director in Maryland and Delaware. He holds a bachelor's degree from Shippensburg University, Pennsylvania; a master's degree from West Chester University, Pennsylvania; and is fully certificated in school administration in Delaware and Maryland. Chet has negotiated dozens of collective bargaining contracts and has handled hundreds of teacher grievances over the years. He has also conducted professional seminars in the field of teacher dismissal in several states.

DATE DUE

GAYLORD			PRINTED IN U.S.A.